The Lure
of the Falcon

GERALD SUMMERS

DRAWINGS BY DUNCAN MCLAREN

COLLINS
St James's Place, London, 1972

William Collins Sons & Co Ltd
London · Glasgow · Sydney · Auckland
Toronto · Johannesburg

First published 1972
© Gerald Summers 1972
ISBN 0 00 211483 6
Set in Monotype Caslon
Made and Printed in Great Britain by
William Collins Sons & Co Ltd Glasgow

Chapter I

WE all know how, at an early age, one can be bitten by the bug of some enthusiasm, which is normally short-lived but can sometimes last a lifetime. This happened to me; but it wasn't a bug – it was a mongoose. Lhoni was an Indian grey mongoose, a real Rikki Tikki Tavi mongoose, who had ruled my grandmother's household for nearly twelve years. Lhoni had a passion for beds; whose bed it was mattered little, so long as it was warm, soft and accessible. I cannot actually say that I remember what happened as I was only three at the time, but I have heard the story so often from my family that it seems as vivid in my memory as many more recent experiences. I know that I was being put to bed, suffering from flu, which seemed particularly virulent in the years following the Great War. Lhoni, who was already installed between the sheets, objected to this invasion of her sanctum and her teeth met in my big toe. I believe from that time onwards we became almost inseparable.

Lhoni herself was a legend in the family. My grandmother had reared her from kittenhood in India, and wherever my grandparents went, there for the next fourteen years went Lhoni. She was an endearing tyrant or a confounded nuisance, according to whether she happened to like you or not; but no matter how fond of you she might be, she would bite you to the bone without the slightest compunction if she felt that way. My grandparents used to travel extensively on the Continent, and of course Lhoni accompanied them. Like all mongooses, she was a born escape artiste; where her small sealing-wax nose could go, her fluid pepper-and-salt body and brush-like tail could follow. Many a time would she dematerialise in some smart hotel bedroom to appear later in the kitchens or dining-room, to the terror of the staff or delight of the guests, whence she would be retrieved, kicking and chattering with wrath, by her owners who had by now become happily fatalistic about the whole thing. How she survived six months, let alone fourteen years, only the protecting spirit of mongooses knows; but survive she did, to create a record for longevity which I believe has yet to be broken.

Fond of her as they were, my grandparents at one time decided that a mongooseless life was the life for them, and took her at considerable expense back to the jungles of the Central Provinces of India in the hope that Lhoni would mate with a wild mongoose and return to that state for which nature had designed her. But Lhoni had other ideas. Although apparently delighted to be back in her native land, and although she did indeed absent herself for some days, on the very afternoon before her foster parents were due to leave for Bombay and home, up she popped! She obviously wanted to make it clear that the jungle was all very well for a holiday, but that it did not compare with the joys of rural Hampshire or the fun of hunting English rabbits, let alone good regular meals and the pleasure of curling up at the foot of a warm English bed. Besides, she happened to like her adopted family and meant to see them through to the end. So back she came to Britain, and a good many more years of her well-meaning, mis-spent life.

My grandmother had a passion for exotic pets, including a Kashmir blackbird, which incidentally nearly expired whilst passing through the Red Sea on the journey home. Her devoted and long-suffering personal maid and companion, 'Nanny Hill', spent hours spraying it with cold water and was successful in keeping it alive throughout the voyage. She also had at one time a thriving colony of what she called desert mice, but which were, in fact, gerbils. These were attractive little beasts, with warm honey-coloured fur, squirrel-like tails, and placid dispositions. They were, however, a bit of a comedown after the irascible but affectionate Lhoni.

At this period my parents were away in British Somaliland, where my father was Governor and Commander-in-Chief. My sister Anne and I were left to the tender mercies of a large family of maiden aunts, who appeared to live in small colonies scattered about Sussex; they took it in turns to look after us, and very well they did it too. My favourite aunt was Aunt Maud, who at this time was living at Goldstrow Farm, near Piltdown, where the Piltdown man was supposed to have originated. She was a good ornithologist, and I always feel that she imbued me with the love of natural history which has been my lodestar in all the years that followed.

Aunt Maud had an enormous bicycle, first cousin to the penny-farthing; from the handlebars was slung a pannier in which I used to ride, and on sunny summer afternoons we would set out in search of adventure. With Aunt Maud vigorously pedalling we would weave through the dusty Sussex lanes in search of yellowhammers, woodpeckers and nightingales. One of the high spots of these expeditions came when we found the nest of a pair of red-backed shrikes. The dapper little chestnut, grey and pink cock, with his piratical black eye-stripe, made a great impression on me. We found their larder, a motley collection of cockchafers, fledglings and small lizards, impaled on thorns nearby. This was my first experience of the innocent ruthlessness of the wild, and Aunt Maud calmly explained what it all meant, rather than bursting into a paean of rage about the cruelty of the little predators.

My aunt slept in a large sunny room overlooking a glorious, old-fashioned tangle of a garden, full of hollyhocks, snapdragons, wallflowers, Canterbury bells and all the other old English garden flowers, which are so seldom seen these days as everyone appears to have a passion for orderliness. Below the bedroom window was a wall, thick with wisteria, clematis, honeysuckle, and anything else that could creep or climb, and where, incidentally, I once found an old wren's nest full of dormice. Huge orange and black fuzzy bumblebees used to find their way in through the open casements and drone sleepily about the room, where I lay, supposedly enjoying my afternoon rest. This room was divided by a magnificent Victorian screen, covered in pictures taken from old scrap-books, Christmas cards and crackers. Among the haphazard medley of fat, arrogant robins, kittens and mid-Victorian skating parties, was one picture which may well have had more effect on my mind than I realised. It was a splendid likeness of a goshawk which had just made a pass at and missed a rabbit, whose hind quarters could be seen disappearing into a burrow. I can see that goshawk to this day, her raised crest and splendid topaz-coloured eyes, her huge yellow foot with its bayonet-sharp talons reaching for the rabbit's scut, and her great rounded wings half open as she hurled herself against the bank. I am sure that this picture fired me with a love of, and admiration for, all birds of prey, which has grown stronger as the years pass by.

Unhappily this aunt, who had done so much to inspire me with a love of nature and untamed places, and to whom I am for ever grateful, was soon to be taken from me. One day we were going by bus to a little village at the foot of the South Downs, where we had been told there was a barn owl's nest in the tower of the Saxon church. My aunt crossed the road to post a letter, was hit by a motor cycle and died in hospital the same evening. I was packed off to London, numbed with loneliness and a sense of loss, to my grandmother's house in Eaton Place. My father had been wounded in the campaign against the 'Mad Mullah' of Somaliland, and my mother was busy nursing him, so it was, I suppose, natural that I should be handed over to my grandmother who, unfortunately, for all her love of animals, neither understood nor had time for small boys.

I then came under the dominion of a series of governesses, each one more impossible than the last. One in particular I shall always remember, for she used to lock me in my room at the top of the lofty Victorian house, with its endless staircases, which seemed to a little boy of five to climb upwards for ever. She would leave me for hours on end after first telling me, for reasons of her own, that the house was on fire. My grandmother was indifferent to my yells of terror, and the servants, though sympathetic, were too scared of the governess to do anything. My father died in 1925 and my mother, though shattered by her loss, came to collect me and was horrified by what she found. The governess was instantly dismissed, and I, suffering from a nervous breakdown, was put under the care of the well-known child specialist, Dr Truby King, who did his best to get things sorted out for me.

My father, shortly before he died, had bought a house near Horam in East Sussex, and it was to this house that we now moved. Old Acres was an attractive grey-and-white building, with many rooms and an exciting, book-lined passage leading to a large bedroom, which opened on to a balcony guarded by a group of massive Scots pines. Just in front there was an artificial pond, surrounded by rosebeds (my mother was a fanatical rose grower). On the lawns stood a copper beech and a scarlet oak, and below there was a splendid meadow full of scabious, knapweed and ragwort, on which fed the handsome gold-and-black caterpillars of the Cinnabar moth. There was a copse with a huge rabbit warren, and a beech said to be one of the oldest and largest in Sussex. Then there was the stream, a real, slow-flowing Sussex stream, winding its lazy serpentine way to lose itself in the River Cuckmere, which idled across the Weald, finally meeting the English Channel at Cuckmere Haven, some fifteen miles to the south.

'Our' stream, as we always called it, was a paradise to a small boy with a love of nature. In its clear pebble-strewn depths lived gudgeon and loach; huge eels lurked in caverns under the banks, and both brown and rainbow trout could be seen, heads to the current and tails a-flicker as they waited for caddis grubs, mayfly larvae and such-like delicacies to be carried within range of their ever-hungry mouths. Along the banks, overgrown with water mint and other river-loving wild plants, hunted stoats and weasels, ever alert for the scent of water voles, which would plop into the stream with a splash like a falling stone. All I wished for was a companion to share these boyhood thrills. This wish was soon to be granted.

Shifter was a rough-haired hunt or working terrier, of the type now known as a Jack Russell, though in fact bearing little resemblance to the dogs made famous by the Reverend John of that ilk. Whatever his breeding or lack of it, he was just the right companion for me. Shifter had been given to my mother by a school friend of hers who lived in Bath. He had two vices, unforgivable in a

town-living dog: he chased traffic and he fought. With us he rarely showed this truculent side of his nature, but he would tackle any dog that he considered worthy of his attention. His particular enemy was an Irish terrier called Paddy, who lived a few miles away, and these two never lost an opportunity of getting to grips. They were evenly matched and never fought to a conclusive victory one way or the other; however, when they were hard at it neither blows, abuse, nor buckets of cold water had any effect, and they had to be literally choked off each other by judicious twisting of their collars. But Shifter, despite his canicidal tendencies, had a great friend, another hunt terrier called Mac, belonging to the local land agent, Major Tuppn. These two would visit each other's houses and trot off happily side by side, bent on a day's illicit rabbiting. Luckily, despite a local infestation of surly gamekeepers, traps and poison, they never came to any harm.

Shifter was a great character and an ideal dog for a

boy, taking part in all our expeditions both on foot and by bicycle; at this time, and later during school holidays, I seldom went anywhere without him until his death in 1938. His rather off-beat personality was shown when my mother was watching the changing of the guard at Buckingham Palace. After the ceremony Shifter stood eyeing one of the newly posted sentries, an enormous Grenadier guardsman. Something about the man's appearance must have offended him for he suddenly darted forward and seized the guardsman by the trouser leg, shaking and worrying it vigorously. The sentry showed great control; without glancing down he shook the dog off and continued pacing his beat, ignoring my mother's embarrassed apologies. Seeing a policeman bearing down on her, my mother grabbed Shifter, dived into her car and drove rapidly away.

Our cat, Jyx, named after the Home Secretary, Joynson Hicks, was an immense tom, with the colour, the temperament and, as it seemed to me, almost the size of a black panther, combined with the curious hind legs and bouncing action of a lynx. He was a mighty hunter, forever bringing home his trophies, which varied from a half-grown leveret to a large and still very active stoat, all of which would be dispatched to an accompaniment of horrible jungle noises in the inky recesses of the telephone cupboard beneath the stairs. He had a great reputation for ferocity, but it was much exaggerated; at least, on the few occasions when he was neither hunting nor mating, he would sleep the sleep of the exhausted just, tucked up at the foot of my bed, his powerful ribs gently rising and falling, as he purred like a contented lawnmower. His hunting came in useful to me later on when I kept young owls and hawks, as he never failed to keep me well supplied with voles and woodmice, moles and shrews, none of which came amiss to my clamorous and rapacious foundlings. Alas, Jyx's stay with us was short, probably ending in violent death, as one morning he failed to return from his nocturnal marauding, and was never seen or heard of again. This upset the family for a long time, as Jyx for all his evil ways was a great personality, leaving a wide gap in our lives which no other cat could fill.

In 1927 I acquired a new governess, Miss Ena Anderson, who had much influence on my life. She was a keen naturalist, a most unusual thing in those days, and had a passion for collecting and breeding butterflies and moths. She installed a number of glass-fronted wooden boxes on shelves all round our playroom, and these were soon filled with a miscellaneous assortment of caterpillars, ranging from the hairy red-and-black larvae of the Yellowtail moth to the huge horn-tailed monsters which, if we were lucky, eventually buried themselves in soil at the bottom of the breeding cage and weeks later emerged as the perfect insects of Privet or Eyed Hawk moths. Our gardener, George Chapman, was a real Sussex countryman who used to give us many caterpillars and adult moths. These he referred to respectively as 'Hop Dogs' and 'Howletts,' which, as we later found out, were local names for all such beasts, the only ones by which they were known in that part of the country.

Miss Anderson and I used to go for long country rambles, armed with butterfly nets and collecting boxes, accompanied, of course, by Shifter, who had as much fun dashing through the thickets in search of rabbits, which he seldom caught, as we did in our pursuit of Grizzled Skippers, White Admirals and Silver Washed Fritillaries. We generally brought back something of interest from these field expeditions: a young grass snake, a slow worm, or a batch of caterpillars of the Red Admiral butterfly which fed on stinging nettles. These, when full grown, would suspend themselves like bats, head downward from the roof of their box; their skins would split, and soon splendid golden-tinted spiky chrysalises would appear. These pupae, although apparently dormant, would wriggle indignantly if touched.

I remember the excitement with which I used to watch the emergence of the perfect insect; how the shrimp-like skin would split and the occupant struggle forth, its tiny wings looking like a rolled-up groundsheet on its back. The butterfly-to-be would climb to the side of the breeding cage, which we had already placed to get as much sunshine as possible. There, as we watched, and as the lifegiving warmth caught them, the wings would slowly unfold; and as they unfolded the colour crept into them, becoming every moment more and more vivid. Finally, the insect would climb on to a finger to be carried outside into a patch of sunlight. There, slowly fanning her wings as life crept into them, she would know when they had strength to bear her up and, with no trial flight, would suddenly skim and glide away into the hazy summer meadows beyond the lawns.

At about this time I started a collection of butterflies and moths, which I was to continue for the next ten years or so. We were very lucky, for our part of Sussex must have contained the majority of species of butterflies on the British list, as well as an enormous variety of moths. My mother grew both petunia and tobacco plants, and on more than one occasion I was thrilled to see the ghostly figure, hovering huge and white in the moonlight, of the Convolvulus Hawk moth, a giant with a wing span of four and a half inches, an erratic wanderer from the Mediterranean countries. We used to go for day-long excursions to the South Downs near Lewes, where amongst the lucerne fields could be found drifts of Clouded Yellows and where, on one momentous occasion, I netted the much rarer, much coveted, Pale Clouded Yellow, in reality a poor washed-out edition of its commoner relative.

Higher up among the gorse and the sweet-scented, sheep-nibbled downland grass dwelt the slow-flying Marbled White, and innumerable Blues, Coppers and Burnets. Many happy days were spent here; apart from the drone of bees and other insects busy among the flowers at my feet, the silence was broken only by the songs of linnets and skylarks. Almost every gorsebush had its pair of linnets, and their brief yet not unmusical phrases, together with the never-ending stream of song from the many skylarks high above my head, were a constant delight to me. These two birds have, in fact, always seemed to me to represent the very soul and spirit of the Downlands.

In the field on the opposite side of 'our' stream was a horse pond. This was an El Dorado for myself and my friends of that period; not the least of its attractions being that it was owned by a surly and anti-social farmer, who looked exactly like Mussolini, a characteristic which did little to endear him to the older members of my family. This farmer used to creep up on us when we were busy with net and home-made rod, trying to capture some monster hitherto unknown to science which we were convinced lurked in its iris-fringed and duckweed-covered depths. If he caught us unawares he would lay about us with an ash plant, bellowing the while in what I think must have been pure Saxon.

Despite these terrors, the attractions of the pond lured us back time and again, not least because it contained no less than three species of newt. Commonest of these was the handsome smooth newt, the male of which in courting dress was rather like a tiny dinosaur, with his serrated crest running the length of his back; he was a beautifully marked beast, olive-green with black spotted sides and his underneath the golden-pinkish tint of a newly-opened thrush's egg. The great warty newt, a giant nearly six inches long, was a special prize; he was inky black, except for his stomach which was a brilliant orange spotted with black, and he also sported a rather ragged and untidy crest. Finally there was the palmated newt, smaller than either of the others, less distinctive in colour, but with a curious filament sticking out at the end of the tail, which somehow looked as if its owner had narrowly escaped from the jaws of some predator leaving a portion of his tail behind. In addition to newts this pond contained all sorts of other treasures, ranging from the big black Dytiscus water beetle with its voracious appetite and curious oar-shaped swimming paddles, to the tiny thread-like hair worm, which the locals assured us was really the hair from a horse's tail which, if left alone, would eventually turn into an eel.

Miss Anderson showed us how to set up an aquarium, which I remember was made from an old glass accumulator. Here was arranged an almost perfect cross-section of pond life. Amongst the planted reeds and water mint stalked the water scorpion and dragon fly larvae; here, too, the water spider constructed his tiny silver diving bell, his lair from which he would leap forth to waylay a passing fresh-water shrimp, carry it home, and consume it at leisure.

Chapter 2

At about this time my mother, still deeply shaken by the death of my father, decided to go on a long visit to the Continent. To my delight, Miss Anderson, Anne and I went with her. In those days the motor car, though beginning to make its presence felt, was not the constant noisy menace it is to-day. On a long journey one travelled by train, and very pleasant it was too. Although we must have been away for several weeks, I remember only certain outstanding incidents. I think it was in April that we left Old Acres, as I distinctly remember the narcissi and wild daffodils, known to us as Lent lilies, clustered under the lichen-covered apple trees in a corner of the lawn. We crossed the Channel from Dover to Calais, but this voyage, although exciting, was marred for me by my terror of the ship's fog-horn, which induced me to seek refuge down below, with my hands over my ears. I was eventually found by a friendly member of the crew, who explained to me that the ship was not, as I feared, about to sink, and consoled me by taking me to see the engine-room.

Somehow we found our way to the tiny country town of Ribeauvillé, a glorious place half hidden in the Vosges mountains and straight out of the pages of *The Prisoner of Zenda*. The most noticeable and popular inhabitants of Ribeauvillé were the storks — as the ravens are to the Tower of London and the apes to Gibraltar, so were the storks to Ribeauvillé. It seemed that every large building from farmhouse to parish church had a stork's nest, built on a cartwheel put there for the bird's convenience. These storks fed in the fields and marshes surrounding the town and would come sailing in just above the rooftops with their necks and long legs extended. They had a curious prehistoric look about them, almost like friendly ptero-dactyls. They must have had a considerable effect upon the economy of the town, as every shop was festooned with beautifully made papiermaché storks in all sorts of natural and unnatural positions. Another source of local income seems to have been from the sale of musical boxes, whose tinkling notes were derived from a local waterfall, blessed with the lovely name of La Carola. I also recall that many shops sold attractively-made dolls, replicas of Alsatian peasants in national costume.

The town of Ribeauvillé was surrounded by a splendid medieval wall, covered with moss and inhabited by lizards whose curious bird-like feet enabled them to shoot up the perpendicular surface of the wall and dodge into crevices with fantastic agility. I was never able to catch one, despite an ingenious method of fastening my mother's paint mug to a stick and using it like a butterfly net.

Far above the town loomed a magnificent castle, poised like a raven's eyrie on its rocky ledge. A steep craggy path led towards the castle, on one side of which was a tangle of undisciplined vegetation, great clumps of old

man's beard, and almost impenetrable thickets of haw-
thorn and other sharp-thorned guardians of the wooded
slopes beyond. Here one could always find a colony of the
most beautiful beetles I have ever seen. About the size
of small cockchafers, but of an almost indescribable
golden-bronzy green, they were here in dozens, clinging
to the bushes or ambling determinedly through their own
grassy jungle in the curious singleminded way that some
beetles have. They appeared to be confined to a comparatively small area, but how they came to be in that
one favoured spot, and what they were doing there, we
never found out.

My mother and Miss Anderson spent much of their
time sketching, and I was often left alone to explore.
One morning I slipped away and made for the banks of
the little stream beneath La Carola, which was a limitless
source of exciting small beasts; crayfish lurked under the
stones, and it appeared to be the communal feeding-
ground of all the local storks which, being at least as tall
as I was and privileged guests, took little notice of me
and went on with their job of stabbing and pouching
small frogs and other unlovely delicacies for their growing
youngsters, housebound on their cartwheel nests in the
town far above. I was about to work my way back to the
inn, to see if my family had returned, when I noticed a
most unpleasant smell. With the curious mixture of
horror and fascination, not unusual with small boys, I
followed my nose and pushed my way through a screen
of bushes into a clearing. There lay the bloated corpse
of a dog, but I felt no revulsion at the sight – indeed, I
scarcely noticed it – for right in the centre, with its
magnificent wings gently fanning, sat a splendid male
Purple Emperor, one of the most sought-after prizes on
the British butterfly collector's list!

Half paralysed with excitement, I crept forward, terri-
fied that my shadow, falling upon the feasting monarch,
would alarm and send him flickering into the sky, but

he was too intent upon the heady juices of which no doubt he had taken almost his fill. Excited as I was, I was able to take in the picture of this incredible insect; its huge wings, rich velvety brown with a purple lustre, were half-encircled with creamy white crescents. All this I saw, as I crept forward, my right hand poised; foot by foot I drew nearer, and still the Emperor fed on unalarmed. At last I was balanced to strike, my right hand flashed out, and there, clutched in my sweaty palm, was the prize of a lifetime! Almost sick with the thrill of the chase and its triumphant ending, I ran stumbling over the cobblestones all the way back to the inn. My mother and Miss Anderson were there waiting. Incoherent with excitement and exhaustion, I stammered out the whole story, holding up the Emperor, undamaged, despite the undignified end to his carousal. My mother, and I have never really forgiven her for it, told me to let it go. Almost crying with disappointment and fury I obeyed, and the Emperor, apparently undismayed, soared off to disappear over the rooftops. So ended the saga of the Purple Emperor. My only consolation, on looking back through the years, is that there cannot have been many boys of seven who have caught a Purple Emperor with their bare hands.

A few days after the Day of the Purple Emperor, as I still think of it, we crossed the Rhine near Strasbourg and headed southward to Freiburg at the edge of the Black Forest. Freiburg was another medieval city. For some reason it had no storks, but it did have a zoo, where, incidentally, I met my first barn owl and golden pheasant. As a result I have always thought of both these species as peculiarly Germanic birds. Freiburg was the capital of the Black Forest area, and was surrounded by Wagnerian pine forests, which ought to have been infested with 'wolves and woodcutters,' and where we did, in fact, see our first roe deer, which thrilled me just as much. I shall always remember the furtive reddish grey forms, the buck with his coronet of spiky antlers glancing back over his shoulder, before vanishing in the silent sun-dappled forest, into which they seemed to melt.

There was a lake in the woods a few miles from the city, and once when we went for a picnic it seemed that every toad in south Germany had gathered there. We had to walk to the lake, and while we were still nearly half a mile from it the whole district appeared to be one huge moving carpet of hopping, crawling and shuffling toads, all heading in the same direction. As we drew closer to the banks the air hummed and vibrated with a continuous staccato chorus of croaks, quacks and watery gurgles; soon we saw that the surface of the lake for several yards from the shore was pulsating with a seething mass of toads. It was a curiously repulsive sight. I have always been fond of toads individually, but this was too much of a good thing, and we were only too glad to withdraw and leave this revolting mass of amphibians to their noisy nuptials.

A distant cousin of ours, a Mrs Wilson, had invited us to stay at her villa near Lake Orta in northern Italy, and it was here that we spent the last part of our continental holiday. We broke our journey for a few days in Switzerland, and arrived in Italy via the Simplon Tunnel. This turned out to be a somewhat hazardous trip as my mother nearly landed us in a concentration camp for saying something uncomplimentary about Mussolini and the inefficiency of the Duce's railway system.

Mrs Wilson was a strange, autocratic figure, swathed in lace, and flanked by two enormous Alsatians who rejoiced in the names of Czar and Czarina. These ferocious beasts were rarely far from her side, and added to the air of unapproachability that she cultivated. My cousin had a curious phobia; she could not stand the sound of anyone coughing. This was unfortunate for me since I had contracted whooping cough in Geneva. As I lay in bed, racked with spasm after spasm in the small hours of the morning, she would bellow out from her adjoining room, telling me in no uncertain tones to shut up or at least to keep my head beneath the bedclothes. This did little to endear us to one another, but there were compensations. First of these, I seem to remember, were the swallowtails.

There was a flight of marble steps leading to the garden, and at the foot of these was a group of the finest magnolias I have ever seen. These attracted a host of butterflies, not only the usual Peacocks and Red Admirals but all sorts of Mediterranean species – a kind of Brimstone, like ours but of a warmer, rich, orange-yellow; innumerable Fritillaries; and lastly, two kinds of Swallowtails. One was the same as the British species, which is now confined to the fens and marshes of East Anglia; the other was the so-called Scarce Swallowtail, which had bold, velvety-black vertical stripes against a background the colour of Cornish cream. These Scarce Swallowtails were, in fact, commoner than their better-known relatives, and every spray was covered with one kind or the other. They would come sailing in with their deliberate, hawk-like flight, undoubted aristocrats among the smaller, more plebeian, species. They created an impression of disdainful ease with their powerful flight, a quality shared with the Purple Emperor and a few other butterflies, that never fails to thrill me.

One day I found a newly-emerged Scarce Swallowtail drying its wings on a sunny patch of wall near the house, and decided to keep it for a while as a pet. She, for it proved to be a female, was housed in a muslin-fronted meat safe and provided with a sprig of magnolia, pur-loined, I regret to say, without my cousin's consent. In a very short time she would climb on to my finger and uncoil her watch-spring proboscis to sip the juices of a lump of sugar soaked in water. I would hardly dare to claim that she became tame in the accepted sense, but I do know that I could take her out and let her fly about the flowering shrubs in the garden; and I could then, approaching quietly while she was sunning herself on a blossom, induce her to step on to my finger for her ration of sugar water. This she seemed to love above all else, and she was then content to be carried back into the house. One morning I found a cluster of minute, greenish white eggs attached to the side of her cage, so I rather reluctantly decided to let her go, and off she went with no sign of gratitude for the board and lodging she had received.

A few days later, returning from our daily walk along the shores of Lake Orta, Miss Anderson and I came across a lovely salamander, a large newt-like amphibian with an attractive moist skin of a deep sooty-black relieved by irregular patches of fiery orange, which made it look most fearsome, though it was, in fact, entirely harmless. Unfortunately the Italians, who should have known better, refused to accept this fact, and attributed all sorts of evil doings to this attractive and interesting creature. I was proudly carrying it up to the front door when Pietro, the 'major-domo,' appeared at the top of the steps; he gave one horrified look and broke into a torrent of hysterical Italian, of which Miss Anderson and I could not understand a single word. At this moment the gardener arrived, attracted by the din; being a man of action, he seized a broom, and before I could take any evasive action swept the salamander off the palm of my hand, where it had happily settled, into the depths of the shrubbery. I do not know who was the more disappointed, Miss Anderson or myself.

As some sort of consolation Pietro produced a card the following morning on which were stuck several hundred silkworm eggs. On arrival home in England these were put into the cupboard under the stairs, and promptly forgotten: some time later my mother, on one of her somewhat irregular inspections, reported that the entire cupboard was alive with tiny black caterpillars. These were rounded up and put in one of our breeding cages where, for want of mulberry leaves, they were fed on lettuce which appeared to act as a satisfactory substitute.

They ate alarmingly, grew apace, and soon fulfilled their purpose. They retired to the floor of the cage and spun like mad, producing delicate golden-silk cocoons; these, sadly however, were never woven into wedding-gowns for fairy princesses, for which I felt sure they were intended.

Chapter 3

O N our return to England my life went on much as before. I roamed the woods and fields collecting newts, field mice and other small creatures, and went with Shifter on long, exciting, poaching expeditions from which we generally returned empty-handed; though on the few occasions that Shifter succeeded in catching a rabbit we came home as proudly as if we had snatched the Crown Jewels.

However, these glorious, care-free days were numbered. One day Miss Anderson came to me as I lay in bed reading one of my favourite animal stories and told me she was going to leave us, that she was going to be married. I felt as if she had betrayed me. What right had she to do this to me? I had assumed, if I had thought about it at all, that she would be with me for ever. I had even toyed with the idea of marrying her myself, not in the least concerned that there must have been at least fifteen years between our ages. I remember the day we saw her off at Heathfield station. None of us spoke much; my mother tried to make her usual bright remarks, though even she was sad at the thought of losing someone who had become very much a part of the family. I felt as if I had been kicked in the stomach, and even the irrepressible Shifter, who was devoted to her, was less exuberant than usual. But worse was to follow. A few days later my mother told me that I was to be sent away to a prep school. At the time the full significance of this did not really sink in, upset as I still was by the departure of Miss Anderson, a companion who had done so much to encourage and help me with my boyish problems and overcome the disastrous effects of the previous governess.

I had not yet entirely recovered from whooping cough, and so I did not begin my school life until at least three weeks of the summer term of 1928 had elapsed. The prep school chosen for me, where my father had also begun his education, was at Forest Row on the edge of Ashdown Forest, not far from East Grinstead. My mother must have discussed my eccentricities with the head-master and mentioned my interest in natural history because, to my surprise and delight, I was allowed to take an aquarium of newts with me! On arrival I met the headmaster and his wife, and the matron, who regarded my collection of newts with ill-concealed suspicion. My precious aquarium and its occupants were handed over to the tender mercies of the gardener, and I was told that I could visit them once a day, to feed them and to change their water. This, I suppose, was better than nothing, but I felt pretty bleak about it at the time. My mother kissed me, told me to be brave, and assured me that the holidays would not be long in coming. She then climbed into Atalanta, our ancient blue Singer, and went clanking and bumping down the drive. I felt as though I had been abandoned, like a castaway on a desert island.

The deputy headmaster took charge of me, led me along endless passages, opened a door and pushed me through into a room where my future school-fellows were assembled. A group of these advanced upon me, like a pack of wild dogs. 'What's your name?' said the leader, a fat red-haired boy of about eleven. 'Leslie,' said I. 'Leslie? That's a girl's name! I say, you fellows, this new squit's got a girl's name!' At this point I made a private resolution to change my name at the first opportunity. 'What's your surname, new squit?' asked my interrogator. 'Summers,' I replied. This brought forth more shafts of wit. 'Does your mother wash?' 'Yes,' I answered almost in tears. 'Then she must be a washerwoman.' And so it went on. Luckily at this juncture a master appeared, and we trooped to the dining-room for tea and biscuits, but I could eat nothing.

That night in my hard, cold bed, sleepless and utterly wretched, I knew the full, terrible pangs of homesickness. At last I dozed off to dream of Shifter and the fun we had together, only to be jerked awake by the school bell dinning stern reality into my unhappy ears. The first few days were a haze of misery, hunger, cold and fear, but I must have somehow come to terms with my new surroundings, for I survived to the end of that term and of several terms that followed. I was not a popular or successful scholar. I found that my interest in nature and living things was regarded with suspicion and that I was looked upon as a dangerous rebel or worse.

At this time the only interest likely to be taken in birds by most people was in shooting them or collecting their eggs, and the idea of simply wanting to watch them, or to keep them as pets, was unthinkable. There must, I suppose, have been budding naturalists about, but I never met any. I remember, however, that I earned a modicum of brief but highly satisfactory respect during my second summer term. One day when we turned up at the swimming bath, which incidentally must have provided a haven for aquatic life, as it was full of newts, frogs and water beetles, a large grass snake had got there before us and was swimming about with great speed and dexterity. Everybody thought it was a dangerous adder, a misconception which I made no attempt to correct. Slipping into the pool I gripped the writhing monster by the back of the neck, and after a suitable display of bravado released it and saw it glide rapidly into a welcoming thicket. My stock went up considerably for a time at least.

Alas, my career at this excellent seat of learning was brief and inglorious. A crisis came towards the end of my second year. There was a small lake in the school grounds, an exciting place fringed with bulrushes and yellow irises, the haunt of kingfishers and dabchicks, where dragon-flies and damsel-flies patrolled, alert for insect prey. I used to spend as much of my spare time there as possible, safe from the prying eyes of authority. There I would sit and dream of home and what I would do in the holidays; with me I always took my inseparable companion, Richard Jefferies' *Bevis*, at that time a great source of comfort and inspiration.

At the end of each term, after the exams were over, there were always a few days of anticlimax before the final, glorious LAST DAY. These were devoted to packing and light-hearted general knowledge tests followed, according to which term it might be, by a conjuring show or a sing-song, anything to keep our idle hands out of mischief. In spite of this there were quite a few periods when we were more or less unsupervised. On this particular occasion I managed to slip away to the lake for a little quiet contemplation of the pleasures to come when, looking up on hearing the sudden, trilling call of a little grebe, I noticed something shining golden-bronze, caught in the leaf-filtered evening sunlight among the reeds on the far bank of the lake. Hurrying round, I found it was an enormous fish, a carp, floating on its back in the murky, shallow water. I broke off a forked branch, and after a good deal of manœuvring, managed to draw the defunct leviathan to the bank, where I grabbed it and hauled it ashore. It was colossal, almost as big as I was. I inserted a hazel wand through its mouth and gills, and feeling like a cross between Jonah and Izaac Walton, staggered towards the school, and the anticipated envy of my fellows. Half-way between the laurel shrubbery from which I had emerged and the boys' passage which was my destination, I heard a bellow from the private lawn, where stood the headmaster himself.

'Come here, Summers! What on earth is that?' he inquired, as I stood cringing before this god-like figure.

'A fish, sir,' I answered.

'So it would appear, Summers,' said he, 'but where did you catch it?'

'In the lake, sir,' I replied, with no real intention to deceive.

'Well, well, congratulations, my boy, it would appear that you have prospects in the piscatorial, if not the scholastic field. We will have it cooked and served for breakfast.'

'Thank you, sir,' said I, and fled. The fish was fastened to a nail on the wall by the boys' entrance, and for an hour or so I basked in the admiration and envy of my school fellows. This was my hour of triumph. I confided the secret only to my one real friend there, a boy called Marriott, and he promised never to disclose the truth of this shameful incident.

At breakfast the following morning the fish, in the

form of a solitary fish-cake each, appeared on our plates, and was attacked by the horde of youthful, human locusts. I looked closely at mine, from which arose a slight, but noticeable, odour: I glanced at Marriott who was busy slipping his into his handkerchief, unobserved by his neighbours. I did likewise, and soon the meal came to an end.

An hour or so later, with luggage packed and ready at the door, we waited for the cars to arrive to collect their respective passengers and whisk them away for two months of bliss. One of the first, thank heavens, was Atalanta with George Chapman at the wheel, his chauffeur's cap set at a jaunty angle, unlike the battered felt he wore when gardening. He helped me with the luggage and I just had time to greet Shifter, who was sitting proudly on the front seat, when I glanced towards the staff entrance. There, advancing upon me, were the headmaster and the matron, both looking decidedly pale about the gills. I sprang into the car and urged George to a rapid departure, and as we gathered speed, lurching wildly down the drive, I glanced back. Two figures were gesticulating in our direction from the top of the steps. I never saw them or the school again. This was the final blow; after two years of undiscovered, if suspected, crime, the powers-that-be decided my presence there could well be dispensed with, and so we parted with little regret on either side. When the inevitable letter came my mother was remarkably philosophical about it and immediately set about finding a new school for me.

The next school was at Rottingdean, near Brighton. Here I was much happier. The headmaster encouraged my interest in natural history, and even lent me books on the subject from his private library. The school library itself was excellent and contained the works of Archibald Thorburn, in my opinion the finest bird artist that Britain has produced. Here I met a boy, Basil Chambers, whose parents were in India and who, I soon discovered, had similar tastes to my own; we became close friends, and have remained friends ever since. He used to spend some part of his holidays with us and the remainder with several uncles scattered about southern England. We had great fun together, sugaring tree trunks at night for moths, rising before dawn to watch the barn owl winging its silent, ghostly way home to roost, and filling our aquarium with an astounding variety of pond life.

We reared an orphan song-thrush fledgling, which we called Sandy, short for Alexander. Sandy was the first bird pet with which I was entirely successful. He was astonishingly tame, living in complete liberty; and though seldom out of the house he would accompany me on expeditions, riding on the handlebars of my bicycle. One day he was accidentally trodden on, and though he was apparently not seriously hurt we took him to the London Zoo for a check-up, where we were congratulated by the curator on the job we had done in rearing him to such robust health.

There was a pet shop in Brighton which sold stick insects, curious beasts whose name exactly describes them. We used to put some of these rather sluggish creatures into the bowl of 'mixed vegetation' which was always the centrepiece of our dining-room table, and enjoy the reactions of visitors when the whole mass of what had been seemingly inanimate foliage suddenly came to life. At school these stick insects proved to be useful currency as barter for cigarette cards and so forth.

One day we discovered a large colony of long-eared bats in the attic, below the roof of Old Acres. I have always been fascinated by bats, and have studied them as closely as possible. The first pet bat we had was called Balbus after a legendary Roman gentleman who, according to our 'Shorter Latin Primer,' was supposed to have built a wall. He was most attractive, with a furry brown body, only about two inches long, and vast trumpet-like

ears which, when he was awake, were perpetually on the move and which he could curl up like rams' horns. These ears were folded back beneath his wings when he was asleep. He had small, bright and friendly eyes, and a prodigious appetite for meal worms, of which he must have consumed at least his own weight every day. He could scuttle about at a fair speed, and he would climb rapidly about my person, using the hooks, which were really thumbs, which protruded claw-like from each of his shoulders when his wings were closed. He could hover like a kestrel, and would dart at and catch in flight any winged insect which was released for his benefit during his daily flying exercise in my bedroom. I took him back to school with me and he proved an affectionate and even intelligent pet, and must have taught a good deal about small wild things and their way of life to many boys who,

34

living in towns, would have no means of making their own observations.

We found other bats in our roof, tiny pipistrelles, the common bat of our villages and farmsteads, and once I extracted from its refuge behind a beam a fine noctule, a comparative monster, at least four inches long not counting the tail, and with a fourteen-inch wing span. This was a handsome foxy-red bat, with a face like a diminutive grizzly, powerful jaws and a temper to match. We kept her loose in a spare room at home, where she spent the day suspended from the curtains. She would climb all over me, take large numbers of cockchafers from my hands and crunch them with her wicked, white teeth. She also enjoyed a drink, which she would lap from a paint brush dipped in water, not, as one would suppose, from a dish. One day, when she had been with us a month or so and had become used to being handled, I noticed that she did not seem quite as active as usual. When I went to pick her up for her usual ration of cock-chafers and meal worms she gave forth a shrill cricket-like chirp of protest, and bit my finger hard. As she obviously did not want to be disturbed, I left her alone with her supper. A few hours later the food was uneaten, and she was holding one of her wings draped round her and not, as usual, folded closely to her side; she was also licking something that she held close to her breast. Later I found out her secret as she was doing her daily cleaning-up operations, hanging by one leg and licking her fur, wings and tail membrane with a minute pink tongue, for she was always as particular about her toilet as a cat; clinging to her breast, with feet, wings and mouth, was a tiny, pink infant noctule, less than an inch long. That evening I left the window open, and in the morning she and her youngster had gone.

The headmaster of Rottingdean School was unusually broadminded, and especially so with regard to compulsory games. Although we had to take part in these, and boys who showed a natural aptitude were encouraged, others, like myself, who hardly knew a cricket bat from a hockey stick, were not regarded as being entirely beyond the pale. The sports master, who also taught English and Mathematics, was equally tolerant. He lived in a room at the top of a turret, which was reached by a flight of winding stone steps; in the walls were little, medieval-looking slits, of the sort used by archers to shoot at a besieging army. Here Mr Taylor had his den, and here I used to visit him officially to discuss the merits or other-wise of my last English essay, or to receive tuition in algebra, at which I was hopeless. The talk often turned to entomology, and Mr Taylor, knowing my distaste for cricket, had an original way of persuading, or rather bribing, me to do my best. It was arranged to our mutual satisfaction that for every five runs I scored I would receive a certain number of moths, and the same would apply if I distinguished myself as fieldsman. He was in a good position to carry out his promise for, after the school lights had been turned out, he would sit reading with an Aladdin lamp for company far into the night; and to his room, drawn by the glow, would come all sorts of exciting moths and other insects, such as Red and Yellow Under-wings, Eyed, Poplar and Privet Hawk moths, and on one momentous occasion a splendid Deaths Head Hawk moth, with its trade mark of a bold, grey skull on its thorax, and a squeak like an angry mouse.

I would not say that this unorthodox method did much to add to my prowess, but it certainly increased my zeal. I must have scored a fair number of runs, for at the end of the summer term I had a collection of British moths to be proud of. My friend Basil and I, together with Micky and Billy Stoop (sons of the late Adrian Stoop, the famous England rugger player) and a few other enthusi-asts, formed a small Natural History Society of our own. We kept young starlings and jackdaws, which used to find their way into the classrooms, to our acute embarrassment. We also at one time or another had hedgehogs, dormice and other less interesting creatures.

There was a tea garden a few miles away at Berwick, which had a small zoo; we used to visit this on Sundays and return with tree frogs and green lizards, so adding a more exotic flavour to our collection. It says much for the good nature and understanding of the whole staff that they tolerated us and our varied menagerie for a week, let alone two whole years. Despite all the outside attractions, I managed somehow to scrape through the Common Entrance Exam, as a reward for which my long-suffering mother presented me with a large and handsome European water tortoise, a pleasant, friendly reptile, which lived for some years in the small pond on our lawn.

Chapter 4

BRADFIELD COLLEGE, where it was decided I should continue my studies, is one of a number of public schools which were built in the middle of the nineteenth century. It stands, a scattered group of grey, creeper-covered buildings, beside a tributary of the Thames, not far from Reading. It is surrounded by low-lying farmlands, water meadows, and by deep, clear, slow-flowing Berkshire streams, the haunt of trout, grayling and water voles. It was a typical public school of the old-fashioned sort when I arrived for the winter term of 1934. The good old maxim of sparing the rod and spoiling the child prevailed. Fagging, beatings and a fetish for physical prowess were the order of the day.

Bradfield had two unusual characteristics: it was a soccer, as opposed to a rugger, school, and it had an open-air theatre in which Greek plays were performed every second summer term. These plays took place in a replica of the real thing, complete with tiers of stone seats, which had been built in a wooded dell close to the Sanatorium. The plays themselves were memorable and were always well acted by senior members of the school, and sufficiently enthralling to make one forget the torment inflicted on one's person by the legions of midges that descended the moment one was seated. I survived the faggings and the beatings with no lasting effect on my character, and I managed more or less successfully to keep out of the way of prefects, who virtually ran the place. The only tyranny impossible to escape was the obsession with games and other physical activities.

When I had been a member of the house for a few days I, together with a dozen or so other new boys, was ordered to report for an interview with the head of the house, an Olympian figure, who was not only responsible for discipline within the house, but also happened to be captain of cricket, football, and practically everything else as well. As we trooped into his study he looked at us with a distaste which he made no attempt to conceal. Having disposed of my companions who, it appeared, had represented their respective prep schools in one team or another, he came at last to me. 'Do you play cricket?' he asked.

'Very little, sir,' I answered, almost speechless with embarrassment.

'Call me Dobson, not sir,' he remarked. 'Do you play football?' he continued.

'Not much, Dobson,' I replied.

'Well, what the devil do you do?' he said, peering at me as if I was a particularly obnoxious microbe.

'I can box,' I replied in desperation; anything was better than this verbal dissection, and I had done a little boxing at Rottingdean.

'Right!' said he ominously, 'we'll soon see what sort of a show you can put up; you can go now!'

I was not kept long in suspense. The very next afternoon I, together with one or two other unfortunates, was

39

told to report to the gymnasium. As I drew aside the musty curtains which, for some unexplained reason, hung just in front of the door, I noticed a mountainous thug shadow-boxing in a corner. At that point I wished to heaven I had opted for hockey, fencing or anything rather than this. However, I still hoped; perhaps he was not to be my opponent after all. But luck was against me. After my fellow gladiators had been put through their paces and had all survived with honour more or less intact, it was my turn, and of course it was the man mountain who climbed into the ring to oppose me. Feeling all the conventional symptoms of terror and a good many more besides, I followed suit.

After the usual patter from the college sergeant-major about making it 'a good clean fight, etc.' the bell went for the first round. King Kong put up his fists and came after me. I danced round him looking for an opening. For a fraction of a second he dropped his gloves and I hit him twice; he shook his head and came after me. I got in once more and danced away, but still he followed after me. I got in a beauty with my right; King Kong grunted, shook his head, and came after me again – his left flashed out like a piston and when I came to I was lying on a coconut fibre mat, with King Kong and the sergeant-major bending over me. King Kong looked perplexed, the sergeant-major was grinning; 'That'll learn you to keep your guard up,' he said. King Kong, whose real name turned out to be Dennis, put out a hand like a leg of beef, hauled me to my feet and dusted me down. We became close friends.

The term came eventually to an end, and I went home for the Christmas holidays with a feeling of some satisfaction at having survived my first term at a public school. In that part of East Sussex we were a fairly close-knit community; all the local families seemed to know each other, and we were always visiting each other's houses. The younger people used to give dances, tennis parties, picnic parties, bathing parties, and just parties with no particular end in view, except to enjoy ourselves.

Then there was the Pantomime. This was the special brainchild of a retired brigadier who, aided by his wife, was the organising genius of a great deal of our social life. It was based on the story of Ali Baba and the Forty Thieves and nearly all the young people of the district were dragooned into taking part either as actors or in some connection with the stage management. We used to turn up dutifully for rehearsals and had a lot of fun out of it. Unfortunately the performance – there was only one – coincided with a particularly devastating outbreak of flu, which wreaked havoc among the cast. Finally we were reduced to about a dozen, which luckily included Ali Baba himself, Cassim and the leading lady, Morgiana, who was played by the most attractive of our local lovelies. When the great evening arrived, the audience, twittering with anticipation, settled into their seats. The village schoolmistress, seated at a very ancient and asthmatical piano, struck up a rousing tune, and the curtain rose to disclose the cast in all their borrowed or home-made glory. There, surrounding the principal *dramatis personae*, were four ferocious robbers, the lights reflecting the enormous fake diamonds in their multi-coloured turbans, their teeth flashing evilly in their swarthy walnut-stained faces, each brandishing aloft a wicked-looking cardboard scimitar. From the neck of each robber hung a large cardboard sign which bore the legend 'I REPRESENT TEN THIEVES.'

I spent two years at Bradfield, during which I had my first introduction to falconry. One Sunday evening in July 1935 a friend of mine who was in the Scouts returned from a weekend camp on Bucklebury Common. With a great show of secrecy he hurried me to the special place, behind the science labs, where we kept our surreptitious collection of pets; upending the sack which he had carried slung over his shoulder, he carefully shook the contents to the floor, and stood back waiting for my reactions. There, her grey-brown, down-flecked wings half raised, her formidable talons at the ready, and her marigold eyes glaring hate at us, was a half-fledged female sparrow hawk. This was a prize indeed. I stood gazing at her for some minutes. 'Crikey, what a beauty!' was all I could say. I attempted to pick her up. She fell over on to her back and grabbed my hand with both feet. The grip was almost frightening in its savagery. Her beak was open and she hissed like a scared kitten. I drew back my hand rapidly; she came with it and it took some skill to detach her convulsively gripping talons without hurting her.

We had an empty rabbit hutch recently vacated by Loppity, the leveret we had rescued. Here we installed our new acquisition on a comfortable bed of dry leaves. I hardly slept that night. The next morning before early school we rushed up to our hideout and fumbled madly to open the door of the hutch. There she was, as fierce as ever, and beside her lying amongst the leaves was a small oval pellet which she had cast during the night. Luckily there was a butcher in the village, and during break I called there and for sixpence of my none too plentiful pocket-money bought a piece of tender steak. I picked up the eyas sparrow-hawk on my return and, in spite of getting well clawed, managed to open her neat little hooked beak and slide small pieces of the meat over her tongue to the back of her throat; thus she took her first cropful of meat with us. I bought a number of mousetraps and so was able to provide a satisfactory substitute for small birds.

I had always known vaguely that hawks had been trained for hunting, but had given the matter little thought and had assumed that the sport had died out in the Middle Ages. I possessed only one book that even mentioned the subject, a fascinating volume called *Country Pastimes for Boys*, which had been published towards the end of the nineteenth century. It contained much esoteric information ranging from a recipe for making birdlime to the art of tickling trout, and included a section on falconry, with illustrations taken from Lascelles' *Art of Falconry* in the Badminton Library.

We called the young sparrow-hawk Jessica, for no better reason than that we were doing *The Merchant of Venice* at that time, and somehow the name seemed to suit her; she became tame very quickly and grew almost as one watched her. We were able to get a number of small birds for her, mostly casualties picked up from the sides of the road. We had fitted her with jesses, the light leather straps that all trained hawks wear on their legs, and when she could fly we let her go wherever she wished. She remained free, or 'at hack,' for about three weeks. During the period of hack I always made a point of feeding her on the fist at regular intervals whenever my scholastic duties permitted. Thus she was more or less tame when the time came to train her. She quickly learned to come a long way out of a tree straight to the fist, and she was remarkably steady or well manned. I carried her on my gloved fist wherever I could and she attended a number of cricket matches where, I regret to say, her presence distracted a considerable amount of attention from the game. She would feed happily with a huge crowd of boys standing around her, and I must confess I thoroughly enjoyed the reflected glory that she shed upon me. One day, quite unexpectedly, she left my fist like a tornado, dashed low across an open piece of ground, and seized an unsuspecting young blackbird. She was now 'entered' to quarry.

I took her home for the holidays, and she behaved very well. My mother was at first inclined to look upon Jessica with suspicion, but soon learned to respect if not exactly to like her. I received many invitations from land-owners who wanted to see what she could do, and she seldom let me down. At the end of the holidays I took her back to Bradfield, where she was now officially regarded as part of the establishment. Shortly after I returned I attended a lecture given by Captain Knight, who was accompanied by his golden eagle, Mr Ramshaw. After the lecture I had a long talk with Captain Knight and introduced him to Jessica; he gave me a lot of advice and encouragement, and from then on I was, and still am, a confirmed falconer. Jessica took eighteen head of quarry before finally becoming lost whilst in pursuit of a mistle thrush, a tricky quarry at the best of times. This wasn't a bad effort for the first hawk I had ever trained.

One of the great things about public school life was the comparative freedom we enjoyed and the fact that we were regarded as reasonably responsible beings. In our spare time, of which we seemed to have a great deal, we were allowed to go more or less where we liked. Most of us had bicycles, and these greatly increased our range of exploration. There was a small group of us who, though belonging to different houses, were brought together by our common interest in nature. We used to travel far afield, and on half holidays and Sunday afternoons we would set off for Bucklebury Common, where we once found a hobby's nest and watched the parent falcons bringing dragonflies and small birds to their growing brood. We would lie on our backs in the deep, sweet-scented grass, admiring the aerobatics of the whole family, airborne at last, cutting up the sky with a speed and grace which made the swifts and swallows look like sluggards. We would go fishing on the Thames at Pangbourne, or explore the water meadows nearby, keeping a lookout for grebes and water-rails. There were the Blue Pools, a curious and beautiful natural phenomenon, where the deep, clear water, set off by its surrounding frame of emerald-green watercress, was a rich cobalt shade.

A few miles from the college was a large estate where a number of gamekeepers were employed and where

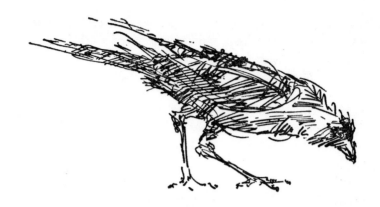

trespassers were not encouraged. On one of our forays here we discovered a large wire trap which had a sort of funnel in the middle; here were imprisoned numbers of jackdaws, rooks and other members of the crow family, attracted by the bait of decaying rabbit meat with which the cage was supplied. We put two or three jackdaws underneath our blazers and released the rest of the prisoners. These jackdaws were taken back to school and, though adult, soon became comparatively tame; and on being released, one of them would return for food for quite a long time. Later we found tawny owls, little owls and even a kestrel in this trap, and released them all.

Belonging to an army family it was natural that I should join the O.T.C. The Corps, as it was generally known, was an integral part of the college life and most of the boys over fourteen were members. The contingent from each house formed a separate platoon, the whole combined unit being the equivalent of a battalion. It was under the command of the housemaster of E House, a fiery, retired major who had been badly gassed in the First World War. We used to turn up each week for parade where we learned the rudiments of arms drill and simple, tactical operations. The high spot of each term was the Field Day, which we used to hold in conjunction with some other school, such as Beaumont, who would act the part of the enemy. At the end of the summer term there was a voluntary camp, which lasted ten days and took place at Tidworth in Wiltshire.

I attended one of these camps at the end of my last term at Bradfield, and for some reason during the course of this had to meet my mother in London. Having no other clothes with me I naturally travelled in uniform, and on my return from Waterloo I fell in with a regular soldier, a real old sweat, who took me, I think, for a drummer boy or something of that sort. I was much honoured to be accepted in such company and listened enthralled to his stories of fantastic exploits on the North West Frontier, and other heroic deeds in which it appeared my companion had taken a leading part. We parted at Aldershot where he got out, leaving me determined to join the regular army at the first opportunity.

I left Bradfield in 1936 at the end of the summer term. In many ways I had enjoyed my life there and it had been an experience which had done me a lot of good. I spent the first weeks of the summer holidays at my grandmother's house in Eaton Place, near Hyde Park. I was accompanied by Jacko, one of the young jackdaws which I had rescued from the trap. He was my constant companion at that time, and though able to fly as strongly as his wild compatriots he never left me. He settled down quite happily in London, and used to take exercise with me in Hyde Park early every morning before too many people were about. He would follow me, flying from tree to tree, and he was soon on reasonably friendly terms with Shifter, who was not over fond of the strange assortment of fellow guests that I forced upon him throughout the years.

Although I was contented enough in London for a short time, I was, of course, delighted to return to Old Acres, and everything it meant to me. There was a wonderful old farmhouse near the village of Horam that looked as if it had stood there from before the Norman

Conquest. It was owned by a Mr Gorringe. One day I called on him in my search for ferrets, which I had long wished to add to my collection. As I walked down the weed-ridden path to the front door I saw a figure watching me from the shadow formed by an angle of the hedge. He wore a shapeless grey felt hat, like an inverted flower-pot. What little of his clothing I could see appeared to have been made out of lichen, and he was enveloped in a magnificent old-fashioned smock. He was grasping a sickle, and from his fiercely bearded face protruded a foul-smelling clay pipe. When I was within a few yards of him I inquired politely where I might find Farmer Gorringe. He took the pipe from his mouth, cupped his right ear with the appropriate hand, and shouted 'Wot say?' I repeated my request. He put his lips within an inch of my ear, 'Oi be mortal deaf,' he roared. On my repeated inquiry, he drew himself up, pointed a thumb in the general direction of his chest and thundered, 'Oi be Gorringe, Oi be!' I explained the reason for my visit. 'No, I ain't got no verrets 'ere,' he replied, to my acute disappointment.

After that conversation, if it could be described as such, considering he could hardly hear a word I said and that I understood even less of his replies, I managed to explain how much I admired his house, which was in fact just a large cottage. He waved me towards it and showed me round. It was fantastic, all vast oak beams, and floors that undulated like the swell of the sea. An oak staircase bulged out at all angles and led to a loft which ran the whole length of the cottage. Here was a multi-coloured flock of pigeons which, left to multiply as they wished, must have numbered scores. They were led by a heavily-wattled blue cock, which his owner told me was at least twenty years old.

In the deeper recesses of the loft, where the light hardly penetrated, I saw a white ghostly shape, then another, and another; barn owls! It appeared that this had been

their home and here they had bred, one generation suc-
ceeding another, since time immemorial. Old Mr Gorringe, unlike many of his contemporaries, loved the owls
and would not have them disturbed. He knew they did
only good, and was most indignant when I, in my
ignorance, suggested that they might kill the occasional
pigeon squeaker, which it appeared they completely
ignored.

I talked to Mr Gorringe for some time and found that
after a bit we could understand each other fairly well. It
appeared that he had never been in 'one of them new
fangled motor cars' and had no intention of accepting a
lift in ours. He was content, as his forbears had been, to
tramp with his farm stock to the weekly markets at Lewes
or Hailsham. He was a thoroughly happy man, such as
we to-day might envy. He had all sorts of curious ideas,
and was as superstitious as an African tribesman. He
believed that a snake's skin, newly dried and worn
under the hat, was a certain cure for headaches, and that
to prevent the onset of rheumatism all one had to do was
to carry a dead shrew mouse in one's pocket. He practised
these beliefs himself, and judging by his own appearance,
for he was a splendid old man of over eighty and with a
physique to be proud of, his faith must have borne
results. Although he had no ferrets he did give me a pair
of pigeon squeakers, which proved to be the forerunners
of a large and thriving colony, and gave me another life-
long interest.

Chapter 5

In September 1936 I went to Gordonstoun. My mother
had recently heard great things of this school and it was
decided that the sort of curriculum offered there would
best suit my wayward attitude to life, as I had not proved
an overwhelming success at Bradfield either scholastically
or in the playing-fields.

Much has been written about Gordonstoun, which
was founded by Kurt Hahn in the 1930s after Hahn had
been forced to leave his native Germany for making some
forthright remarks about the horrors of bringing up
German children to be a generation of young barbarians.
Gordonstoun House stands in a hollow in the hills, a mile
or less from the Moray Firth, close to Lossiemouth, and
about six miles from Elgin, the nearest sizeable town. It
was for years the seat of the Gordon-Cumming family,
and it was here that Sir Roualeyn Gordon-Cumming, one
of the greatest of the nineteenth-century explorers and
big game hunters, spent his boyhood. It has the reputation

of being the healthiest spot in Britain. I would prefer to say it perfectly exemplifies the phrase, 'The survival of the fittest.' In other words, if you can stand it you can stand anything. The school, an ancient Scottish baronial country house complete with dungeons, is exposed to the full arctic blasts of wind sweeping in across the North Sea from Scandinavia and beyond. I am not surprised that Sir Roualeyn chose Africa for the seat of his operations. Hell itself would have been a joyful relief after the rigours of a Gordonstounian January.

I had been given permission to bring Jacko the jackdaw with me, and this made a great deal of difference for me. Having such an amusing and friendly pet soon broke the ice, and I quickly made friends with those boys whose tastes were similar to mine. Jacko was a great character, as clever and affectionate as a dog, and the fact that, although fully winged, he made no attempt to leave me, lent me a certain air of mystery which I found highly gratifying. After twenty-four hours confined in an aviary, which had been constructed to await his arrival, he was given his full liberty. When not sitting on my shoulder or wrecking my study, he was very happy playing about the school grounds until my release from the classroom. He made friends with MacDonald, the head gardener-cum-porter, who used to feed him with big fat lob worms and bits of his own lunch-time bread and cheese.

As at Bradfield we had bicycles and used to roam far afield; to the Culbin Sands, with its half-buried forest, to the shores of the Moray Firth, and to the little fishing village of Hopeman, a few miles from the school. Sometimes at weekends we would go farther afield to the mountains of the central highlands, those mountains whose dark and lowering heights held a strange attraction for me. Here I had my first view of Britain's wildest, most untameable native: the magnificent wild cat; here I heard the mewing call of the courting buzzards as they wheeled above my head; here, too, could be seen the shy dotterel, and most haunting of all, the wild melodious bubbling whistle of the whaup or curlew could be heard, as true a harbinger of spring in these wild places as is the cuckoo in the south. On most of these excursions Jacko would accompany me, sitting on my shoulder, or balancing with half-extended wings on the handlebars of my bicycle, which had been padded to give him a grip and to save him from the chill of the naked metal.

I shared a study with two or three other boys in the 'Round Square,' a curious circular, almost Colosseum-like building which had, according to legend, been built that shape by an early Gordon-Cumming so that the devil could not catch him in a corner. One of my room-mates was a colourful character, Pat Whitehead, who should have been a professional poacher; what he did not know about ferrets, lurchers, trapping and the ways of wild animals wasn't worth knowing. He gave me a young polecat ferret bitch, which he had bred at the school; she was a joy to handle, friendly and playful, but not above giving one a sharp nip if she felt so inclined. We entered her to rats, of which there was a large colony in some pigsties belonging to the school, and she never failed us, showing all the courage in the world. When released from the bag in which she was transported to the hunting field she would dive underground, and she seldom failed to account for one or more of the enemy, some of which must have been considerably heavier than she was. Another boy had an elderly sheepdog called Bess, and she and Miss Fitchett, the ferret, must between them have reduced the rodent population by scores.

Gordonstoun was a new and entirely different experience from Bradfield. Whereas the majority of conventional public schools at that time appeared to look upon the pupils, probably with some justification, as potential criminals or law-breakers, and one lived more or less continually under the threat of corporal punishment, at

Gordonstoun this was not so. A boy was put on his honour and expected to behave, and if he did commit a breach of discipline he was expected to confess this voluntarily. The prefects, known as colour-bearers because they wore a strip of purple tape like a medal ribbon on their breasts, used to come round at night and ask each boy if he had done his 'Duty,' which was a task allotted to him every day and might consist of such menial work as picking up paper or cleaning out the stables. It was at such a time that we were supposed to own up about any minor disciplinary lapses we might have committed.

The system of punishment was strange too. For a minor offence, such as dodging the daily cross-country run or avoiding the cold shower that followed, one was sentenced to Punishment 1 or 2, which was to arise at dawn and walk a certain distance before breakfast. As far as I can remember, No. 1 involved a walk of a mile or so to Duffus House, where the younger boys stayed until old enough to move on to the main school. No. 2 was a walk of about two miles to the coast guard station, which in stormy weather was manned by the school Sea Scouts. I was a regular candidate for these, generally for such heinous crimes as losing my school books or being late for class. I must confess that once the shock of the actual rising was over I quite enjoyed the walks. I used to collect Miss Fitchett and whistle up Juno and Bess, and on my way I would turn the ferret loose in one of the innumerable rabbit burrows with which the area was pockmarked. I would then spend some exciting moments waiting for the coney to bolt and be pursued by the yapping Bess who was, however, far too old and portly to catch anything. It would dash across the open hillside to the cover of the nearest gorse thicket from which it was impossible to dislodge it. This early morning exercise certainly gave me a prodigious appetite for breakfast, which consisted of a choice, not only of the conventional porridge or cereal, but also of a peculiar, though not unappetising, dish called Muesli consisting of oatmeal, fruit and nuts, and vegetation sticking out all over it. It was an acquired taste, but it was not as revolting as it looked once one got used to it.

Another punishment on the agenda was quite different and consisted of a gladiatorial contest in which the boy to be punished played the part of the Christian martyr. If one had committed a real piece of skulduggery, such as breaking bounds when officially gated, it was considered that a stern lesson was needed. One had to fight it out in the boxing ring with a boy who was large or heavy enough to give one a hiding to be remembered. One Sunday, despite the fact that I had been gated for the crime of rising after lights out to study the habits of a family of long-eared owls in an old hooded crow's nest near the school, I decided to bicycle to Forres and spend the afternoon with some friends. On my return I was told by the guardian, or head boy of the house, to report to Mr Hahn's study. There Mr Hahn, after reading the riot act, told me that I had been sentenced to fight in the ring that very evening after supper. He named my opponent-to-be, a boy I particularly disliked. He was considerably older and bigger than I was and had a reputation for being very handy with his fists.

I did not enjoy my supper that evening; however I received a lot of moral support and advice, not only from my own circle of friends, but from complete strangers who appeared to have as little love for this particular boy as I had. I decided that I would at least sell my life dearly. After supper, accompanied by two seconds of my own choice, I duly reported to the gym where this sanguinary encounter was due to take place. I was almost blinded by the lights, and was only half aware of the spectators who included the deputy headmaster, the matron, most of the colour-bearers and a good many others besides, all gathered to enjoy the Roman Holiday. When my gloves were in place I climbed through the ropes into the ring, passing the assembled witnesses as I did so. 'We who are about to die salute thee!' I thought, and realised just how Androcles must have felt.

At the bell I put up my guard and stepped back, to be overwhelmed by a tempest of blows. I heard later that my opponent, the instrument of justice, had boasted that he was going to end the fight within the first round. I covered up as best I could, swaying like a willow before the onslaught, expecting each blow to find its target and end the contest. So it must have continued for a full half minute – the enemy seemed to have at least four fists, all of which were hitting different parts of me at the same time, but half the round had gone by and I was still on my feet. Suddenly the deluge slackened and stopped; I peered from between my gloves and noticed with considerable relief that the enemy was panting. His first shattering attack had failed. I uncovered a trifle and watched him; for a split second he lowered his guard, no doubt wishing to see what effect the punishment he had dished out had on me. As he lowered his fists I stepped forward and hit him as hard as I could, with all my weight behind the blow. He staggered back, nearly losing his balance; I followed up instantly and gave him my right straight in his solar plexus: to my delight there was a round of applause from the ringside seats – the spectators at least were with me. My opponent, light as a dancer on his feet, recovered instantly and came in hard, striking with a succession of straight lefts, one of which got home and cut my lip open as the bell went.

My seconds, amazed that I was still on my feet, did their work well with sponge and towel like professionals, and when the next round started I was feeling a bit more confident. I came out of my corner like an unleashed hound; taking my opponent by surprise I got home twice, once with a good straight right and with a left hook that shook the enemy, and brought forth a roar of approval from the spectators. I looked at my opponent and saw that he was nearly as battered as I was; his nose was bleeding badly, one eye was closing and he was breathing hard. I had a swollen lip, a cut over my left eye, and my ears were singing unpleasantly, but I was still on my feet as the second round ended.

At the start of the third round my opponent had recovered his wind and came in like a whirlwind once more, but I managed to keep out of trouble and he soon began to slow up again. He was obviously puzzled, for he had not expected much opposition, and he had perhaps assumed that the sympathies of the crowd would be with him. Whatever the reason he made a big mistake and dropped his left hand which, being a southpaw, had been guarding his chin. I gave him a left hook, putting everything I had into it, and he went down. I had learned more at Bradfield than I had realised, because as he regained his feet I was waiting for him. I got in a short jab below the ribs that brought his head forward and followed it with an uppercut that laid him on the canvas. The fight was over, though not in the way intended. I was congratulated on my performance and warned not to commit a similar offence in the future. As for the enemy I could not help a sneaking sympathy for him as he withdrew without a word. We neither shook hands nor became firm friends as a result of this encounter.

At this time Gordonstoun had only been established as a school for a very few years, and a fair proportion of the pupils had been drafted from better-known public schools for a variety of reasons. At this period in the school's history one of the most tactless questions could be to ask a boy why he went to Gordonstoun. The pupils included continental royalty and members of some of Britain's most distinguished families. This rather upper-crust society was leavened by the presence of the sons of some of the local farmers and fishermen. Yet this somewhat mixed collection of humanity did, on the whole, get on very well together and formed a miniature democracy that was a good example to the outside world.

Unlike at Bradfield, all sorts of outdoor pursuits were encouraged, including such activities as sailing, riding, climbing and photography. There were even a few couple of bloodhounds. We always suspected that these magnificent beasts were kept in case anyone tried to escape, but this was a gross injustice, for they did, in fact, provide a great deal of sport, and their terrific baying could often be heard at a distance on the normally silent hillsides as they closed in on their quarry, a fleet-footed volunteer who would run a course of several miles before the hounds were laid on to his trail. I took the part of the quarry several times, and it was a heart-pounding experience to hear that wild challenge drawing closer and to see the pursuers remorselessly working out the line, seldom pausing, growing ever nearer and nearer, until they fell upon their prey, who was then overwhelmed and almost thrown to the ground in an ecstasy of affection. I was distinctly glad that I was not a fleeing malefactor at such a moment. The two hounds I knew best, Hamlet and Ophelia, were under the care of Pat Whitehead, who lavished a vast amount of his spare time seeing to their welfare, and very well they repaid it for it would have been hard to find two more splendid brutes.

The system of school work at Gordonstoun was unusual in that we were given a number of tasks at the beginning of each week which we were expected to complete in our own time; although there were normal classes, these were interspersed with periods which could be devoted to any particular subject and provided that the correct amount of work was done satisfactorily everyone was happy. Each boy had a tutor, who was his confidant and adviser both as regards school work and any personal problems that might arise. This system seemed to work out well, and it certainly suited me as it gave me plenty of time to devote to my own hobbies.

My mother had somehow managed to get seats for the Coronation of King George VI and Queen Elizabeth. This was in May and the school had been given a few days' extra holiday in celebration. Our seats were near Westminster Abbey and we had a splendid view. I shall always remember the bands, the massed troops and the pageantry, the crescendo of cheering as the royal carriages approached, and above all the curious feeling, almost nostalgic, of belonging to one enormous family. There were long periods when little was happening, and this time was enlivened for me by a young mistle thrush I had saved from a cat earlier in the year, and which I had had to bring with me for, even on such a momentous occasion as this, it still had to be fed every half-hour or so. I had a tin full of fat earth worms, and every time the thrush, Misty by name, called for food in her chuckling, fledgling voice, I had to open the tin, seize a worm and cram it down her orange gape. Everyone around seemed most intrigued with Misty, who somehow seemed to humanise this rather awesome affair with her innocent, youthful friendliness and complete lack of respect for persons. During one of the pauses between processions Misty, who up to that moment had shown no inclination to fly, was sitting happily on my finger preening in the warm May sunshine. Suddenly she tightened up her plumage, opened her wings, and before I could stop her she half flew, half parachuted, on to the magnificent garden-partyish hat of a lady several tiers below us. Scarlet with embarrassment, I retrieved Misty and returned her to her basket. I must say the lady took it in very good part.

At the beginning of the summer term of 1937 I arrived back at Gordonstoun with Jacko the jackdaw, Misty and Miss Fitchett, a weirdly assorted trio if ever there was one, but who adapted themselves to school life with surprising ease. The exponents of the various outside activities were divided into 'guilds' and took their chosen pursuits very seriously indeed. I had done a certain amount of riding at home and indeed belonged to the local pony club; I had also hunted whenever I had been fortunate enough to stay with my godfather, Colonel (later General Lord) Ismay and his family at Wormington Grange in Worcestershire. I therefore naturally gravitated to the Riding Guild which, in fact, dealt not only with riding but with every aspect of stable management and horse mastership. Believe me, these horses needed much mastering, for a more cantankerous bunch it would have been hard to find outside a Western Rodeo corral.

One day I was mounted on a hard-mouthed chestnut called Gold Flake which, despite my efforts to control him, came up too close to the business end of a mare called Certainty. Certainty was not only naturally irascible but also in season at that time; she lashed out and caught me with one iron-shod, pile-driven hoof and gave me a compound fracture of my right leg. I was taken to Grey's Hospital, Elgin, where I spent the best part of the term. Despite the pain (I had to have the leg reset twice) I have many pleasant memories of my incarceration there. Not only were the staff all that one would expect from their profession and a good deal more besides, but for the first time in my life since I was a small boy I had time to read and think. My mother came up to see me from Sussex and brought me a case full of books. My friends rallied round and soon my erstwhile spotless, private ward began to resemble a cage at the London Zoo. First Pat Whitehead came with Misty (he was looking after Jacko at school); then a boy brought me a goldfinch mule which he had bought in a local pet shop and which sang beautifully. Finally one of the nurses presented me with a young racing pigeon which had gone off course and was exhausted. This bird roosted on top of a locker in the ward, and used to go out of the window and range the streets of Elgin by day, returning regularly for its evening meal, until it must have reorientated itself and flown off home.

On my release from hospital, accompanied by my retinue of tame birds, I was moved to the school sanatorium where I spent the remainder of the term shuffling about on crutches, with my leg covered in much autographed plaster. This, I am sorry to say, did not prevent my attendance in the classroom. I enjoyed the feeling of being a bit of a hero, but this wore off rapidly and I became increasingly frustrated at this restriction of my normal, dubious activities.

We had an aviary, which we had built ourselves on a sheltered piece of ground behind a shrubbery, close to the stables and kennels. Here we kept our ferret hutches as well as our other pets, including some that we had found injured and kept until they had recovered sufficiently to be released. Jacko and Misty, both of whom were allowed to range about at will, used to roost side by side, an unusual friendship between two birds of such totally different temperaments. We used to visit them as soon as we had our showers to give them their first meal of the day. Normally, as soon as they heard our footsteps rustling through the undergrowth, they would start calling a welcome – each in its own particular way – and would fly out to meet us. Jacko would land on my shoulder, tweak my ear and flutter his wings, pretending he was still a fledgling, although he must have been two years old by then.

One morning we had, as usual, prepared breakfast for Jacko and Misty. Cornflakes soaked in milk and a tiny portion of finely shredded raw beef and hard-boiled yolk of egg were their usual ration; they both looked and were as fit and feather-perfect as any wild bird, so this evidently suited them. Probably both of them caught a considerable number of insects to supplement this diet because they were free to come and go, and the only bond that held them was their genuine affection for us. On this occasion, as we came hurrying up with their breakfast, there were no calls of welcome, no small friendly creatures darting out to meet us and to escort us to the lean-to, where they used to roost on a carefully arranged fir branch. Feeling a stab of fear, we rushed forward in the hope that they might not yet have fully aroused themselves. As we came to the shelter we saw, stirred by the early morning breeze, a powder puff of soft, creamy, black-spotted feathers — mistle thrush feathers. Looking closer we saw on the ground in the corner of the lean-to all that remained of Jacko; his head and neck had been eaten away, and his glossy black feathers lay scattered around him, shed in the struggle he had put up for his life. As I stooped to pick him up there was a rustle from a pile of wood shavings and a bloated rat scuttled into the hedgerow.

Both our pets had gone with little to show of what had, only eight hours before, been happy, living creatures, full of joy and vivacity. Pat and I looked at each other but said nothing; there was at that moment nothing to say. On that summer morning over thirty years ago I conceived a hatred for rats and all their ways that has lasted ever since. We borrowed a wire trap from Macdonald, the gardener, and three mornings later we had our revenge. When we came early to the trap it had been sprung and there, shrieking with rage and fear, its hideous yellow teeth gnashing, was the culprit, one of the largest and most repulsive rats I have ever seen.

We swore we would eliminate the entire colony if possible, and the following weekend we went into action. We borrowed Jock, the gardener's smooth-haired fox terrier, a great dog for a rat; we took Bess and a dog called Rough, a crossbred Scottie, with the right ideas regarding vermin, and our entire stock of ferrets, and got to work. The colony was based in the walls af the pig-sties, but there were outlying holes in the bank beneath the hedgerow, which extended for many yards in all directions. Miss Fitchett went to ground first, her tail fluffed out like a bottle brush, and her eyes glinting with the joy of battle; into two other holes went Snowball, a small white jill with the courage of a stoat, and The Gure, Pat's favourite, a tiny ferret who moved with the speed of light. Blanco, a huge and powerful white hob, was kept as reinforcement in case his friends met with stiff opposition underground.

Within seconds a series of squeaks and scufflings announced that our allies were in contact with the foe, and almost immediately a large doe rat emerged at full speed to be immediately nabbed by Bess, who knew just what to do, and did it – fast. Another and another bolted, all receiving swift retribution; one of the terriers killed two of the enemy within as many seconds. Before the afternoon had ended we had between us accounted for nearly thirty of the foe, and at last no more emerged. Out from a hole licking her chops and ignoring a savage bite, which nearly obscured one of her eyes, came Miss Fitchett, followed by Snowball, who was so thickly plastered with mud and clay as to be almost unrecognisable; only The Grue remained deep in the bowels of the earth. We waited in silence for some minutes with no sign of her. Suddenly Jock, the terrier, started giving tongue and marking at a hole far out on the bank; he was digging furiously and biting at roots in his efforts to enlarge the entrance. We seized him and fastened him to a tree while spades were fetched. After half an hour or so of gruelling work we reached our objective. There, her teeth firmly gripping the throat of a giant rat, lay The Grue. Her eyes were shut and she was shaking her quarry with a single-minded ferocity that was almost frightening in one so small. Victory was ours, and we were never troubled by vermin again. After treating Miss Fitchett's eye we returned triumphantly to school for tea. Jacko and Misty had been avenged.

We had no further trouble from rats while I was still at the school. It is possible that the death of our two tame birds, tragic though it was at the time, may have been the cause of saving the lives of our bloodhounds; for at that time it was not generally realised that these vermin are the means of spreading one of the most virulent of all canine diseases, rat jaundice.

With the deaths of Jacko and Misty life seemed pretty pointless for a while. It is hard to explain to those who have never experienced it just how much the companionship of small wild animals or birds, who have happily surrendered their independence to throw in their lot with their human friends, can mean. This is particularly so at an age when such bereavements really do hurt deeply, and the pain seems to grow to the exclusion of all other feelings. The sense of loss continued for many weeks. I had not realised just how much time I had devoted to these birds: now that they had gone the term seemed to stretch endlessly ahead of me, and my spare time became a burden, a void almost impossible to fill. However, I started to read more and took to wandering farther afield at weekends.

I found much solace in long solitary walks along the cliff-tops where the fulmars sailed, riding the gales with rigid wings, their aerial mastery making the gulls look clumsy amateurs by comparison. A few miles from Gordonstoun, lying close to the Elgin road, was Loch Spynie with its ruined castle. Here in winter came thousands of pink-footed geese; here they roosted and from here they would sally forth at night in great skeins, baying like hounds, their far-carrying clamour adding a touch of mystery to the frosty moonlit northern nights.

The science master, a young German known universally as 'Bex,' was a keen naturalist and showed a good deal of interest in our birds and animals. One day we found the nest of a pair of rock doves, the wild ancestors of all domestic and feral pigeons. This nest was on a cliff ledge a terrifying distance above the sea. We used to watch the parents as they came sweeping in, low and fast, just above the waves and then shot upwards to their nesting shelf. They were exquisite little birds, real thoroughbreds with a style and finish quite lacking in their town-bred descendants. When the young doves were well feathered we decided to take one, hand rear it, and find out how it differed in its ways from an ordinary pigeon.

We went to the cliff-top with a red-haired young West Highlander, called McDonald, who could climb like a chamois. I have never had much of a head for heights, but McDonald went first and after a spider-like descent reached the nest and managed to grab one of the squabs: after some cajoling and mockery from McDonald, I managed somehow to clamber down far enough to take the squab from him and hand it up to Bex, who was hanging half suspended from the top of the cliff looking extremely insecure. McDonald and I reached the top without undue hazard and we all returned in triumph.

We fed the young rock dove on soaked brown bread morning and evening. We just opened its soft fleshy beak, which looked exactly like that of a miniature dodo, clearly showing the relationship, and the bread sop was pressed down the throat until the crop was full. Soon the bird, to which for some reason we never gave a name, was weaned and would take soaked corn from the hand. It became extremely tame, would follow us about, and later when strong on the wing would come straight to the hand, from wherever it happened to be, at the sound of a dog whistle. It used to range about all day and return at night, but after some months it took to staying out for days at a time, and finally failed to return. It was interesting to compare this bird with the domestic pigeon; we found it was far quicker in the uptake, it was more intelligent generally, and seemed better able to cope with unexpected circumstances. Later I reared a young stock dove from an egg placed under an old hen homing pigeon, and found much the same thing; both these birds became tamer than their so-called tame relatives.

In the school grounds there were two immense conical

stone 'doo-cots,' which must have stood there since the days when pigeon pie had been a regular part of the diet of the Gordon-Cummings and their dependants; they were probably at times their main source of meat in the days before the shotgun brought all manner of game within the hunter's range. These 'doo-cots' were still inhabited by descendants of the original stock, and oddly enough had not entirely reverted to type as one might have expected. Although the blue-greys outnumbered the others, there were all sorts of chequers and mealies, ranging from red to almost black; and what appeared to be the leader of one flock was a snow-white bird, as wild and alert for danger as any of its neighbours on the storm-beaten coastal crags a mile away.

When I had been at Gordonstoun a few terms I got to know a number of the local families, some with boys at the school. There was one man I remember well, Colonel Dundas, a keen wild-fowler and naturalist who had a large flock of geese – pink feet, grey lag and brent – feeding on his lawn. All these had been slightly injured and were now free to come and go as they pleased. He had an aviary and I was much impressed because he had succeeded in breeding crossbills, birds which I had not ever seen in the wild. These, he told me, were the native Scottish race, confined to the pine forests of the Spey valley. Then there were two dear old ladies, one a keen ornithologist and the other an equally enthusiastic botanist; they were known affectionately to the boys as Flora and Fauna, and there was little they did not know about their part of the country and its inhabitants.

Chapter 6

ALL this time I had given little, if any, thought to the future. Coming, as I did, from a line of forbears most of whom had been members of the Services, it was assumed, at least by my family, that I would follow in their footsteps and in the fullness of time become Governor of some outlandish colony and eventually retire heavy with years and honours. The idea appealed to me not at all. The thought of a life of discipline and self-sacrifice appalled me. If I ever considered what I would do with my life I imagined that I would become some sort of naturalist. Quite how this was to come about never caused me the lack of even an hour's sleep, as I was much too involved with my birds and my ferrets to give much thought to what then seemed an infinity of time stretching ahead of me.

Miss Fitchett had recently given birth to nine young; five were snow-white albinos like their father, the powerful hob, the other four were replicas of their mother, complete with creamy ear tips and black clown-like facial markings. She was a good mother and would stand no interference from anyone. She fed her kittens well and they all grew apace; as they grew they became more attractive and full of fun and mischief, and would come dashing out of their hutch swarming all over me, and would hang in shaking, worrying bunches to my trousers. They would cluck and hiss and go looping through the grass like over-grown woolly bear caterpillars. They were a great success, but did little to further my scholastic ends.

One morning after break Kurt Hahn sent for me. Much as I liked and respected the good 'Herr Doktor,' I must confess that he scared the life out of me. I cannot explain exactly why this should have been, but there was an air of Olympian aloofness about him; one felt somehow that he 'walked with the Gods and heard voices,' and that one might at any time be called upon to make some supreme sacrifice without a moment to consider the consequences.

I knocked at his study door and was bidden to enter. He was sitting behind an acre or so of desk and sliding the fingers of his left hand between those of his right, a characteristic gesture much aped by the boys; it was also regarded as a danger signal, a warning that something untoward was afoot. 'Summers,' he said, as I stood before him. 'You hof becom ferret-minded!' I considered this awesome prospect. 'Always you are ratting! Why the ratting, my poy?' I explained 'why the ratting' as well as I could, but I could see that he was not impressed. The discussion changed to sterner subjects. It appeared that my progress up the scholastic ladder was not all that could be desired. This was true enough. I had not been over-devoted to my books and was inclined to regard the whole educational system with distaste.

Suddenly he asked me outright what I proposed to do with my life because, as far as he was concerned, I had more or less outstayed my welcome. I lamely explained that I had hoped 'to do something with animals.' He pointed out that to get a worthwhile job in the world of Zoology I would need a degree, and that as I had not even passed my school certificate the prospect was less than rosy; and that the only job I was likely to get with my qualifications was an assistant keeper at the zoo. He finally suggested that the best thing I could do was to go to sea as a deckhand, a suggestion which, considering I had recently been almost overcome with nausea whilst watching the film *Captains Courageous*, struck me as the unkindest cut of all. At the end of the winter term of 1937 it was mutually agreed that Gordonstoun had taught me all it could, and complete with Miss Fitchett and two of her youngsters I packed my trunk, caught a train and departed. I returned to Old Acres and to my mother, who through all these years had never lost her faith in me and believed that I would find my métier one day.

During the ensuing Christmas holidays I spent most of the time in Sussex, but paid sporadic visits to London. On one such visit I renewed my acquaintance with Captain Knight and his golden eagle, Mr Ramshaw. I went to the Tower of London, where I much admired the ravens, poor pinioned apologies of the real thing though they were. I went to Cruft's Dog Show, where I particularly admired the Newfoundlands, massive, black, and possessed of a unique blend of dignity and gentleness. More or less subconsciously I determined one day to own a golden eagle, a raven and a Newfoundland. It took me twenty years to achieve the first of these ambitions, but eventually I fulfilled all three. As I write this in January 1971 Storm, our splendid Newfoundland, lies sleeping at my feet; Random, our ten-year-old Spanish golden eagle, is perched on the fence outside the window; and I can hear the conversational barking voice of Croaky Joe the raven who, although ever alert for mischief, is at this moment sitting high up on his favourite perch in an oak tree at the end of the drive, where he can keep an eye on all the comings and goings of our daily life.

My godfather, 'Pug' Ismay, lived in a lovely Cotswold manor house close to the then unexploited village of Broadway in Worcestershire. Later he was to become one of Sir Winston Churchill's right-hand men, and to take an essential part in winning the Second World War. At this time, in the 1930s, Colonel Ismay had an important job at the War Office, but used to spend his weekends at home, riding, shooting and hunting, and generally living the life of a country gentleman, which is exactly what he was. I used to spend a week or two of most of my school holidays at his home, Wormington Grange, which, with its lake, stable-yard and park, is all an English country estate should be. Colonel Ismay had three daughters, Susan, Sarah and Mary. I was more or less the same age as Susan, and at that time we had quite a lot in common, particularly a passion for pets of all descriptions. One of Susan's particular pets was a sparrow called Biddy which she had reared practically from the egg and which I believe lived to reach maturity. There was also an assortment of dogs, which included Godfather's splendid golden retriever Guinea, an ancient wire-haired terrier, and an immensely powerful white bull terrier, with a villainous black patch over one eye, called Boy, who lurked in the stable-yard and whose pugilistic appearance belied his amiable nature.

One of my first visits, when I was about eleven, coincided with the spring concourse of courting toads, similar to that which I mentioned earlier in the Black Forest. Here again the waters of the lake were seething and boiling with toads which must have numbered thousands. Susan and I decided the home life of toads was worthy of closer study, so we collected scores of these reluctant amphibians and installed them on the balcony which adjoined my bedroom. Later, to ensure that the toads had as natural an environment as possible, we dredged the lake with buckets and deposited the resulting slime and squelchy black mire inches deep on the floor of the balcony. This was only to keep the toads happy as Susan explained later to her enraged mother who, on returning from an outing, was, I understand, greeted by the entire household staff lined up in serried ranks and all determined to hand in their immediate notice. We were made to remove the offending batrachians ourselves and to apologise for the dreadful mess we had made. The ruffled feathers of the staff were eventually smoothed, but I doubt if I was ever fully forgiven.

There were extensive cellars beneath the house, which were the headquarters and diurnal roost of a thriving colony of lesser horseshoe bats. These are curious little beasts with rudimentary eyes and a fleshy protuberance from which they get their name, placed just above the mouth, a strange object rather like a tiny hatchet. It is in these bats, and their relatives the greater horseshoe bats, that the system of radar seems most highly developed. They used to hang like huge chrysalids from the roof of the cellar, and even when deep in their diurnal sleep, apparently oblivious to all round them, would on being approached draw themselves up on their long skinny legs as if aware that all was not well. They could fly at full speed about the vaults and underground passages without touching the walls, and were almost impossible to catch even with a dexterously wielded butterfly net.

Much in keeping with the atmosphere of peaceful timelessness at Wormington Grange was a flock of beautiful black-and-white nuns, one of the most ornamental of the so-called fancy pigeons. These lived in a special loft in the stable-yard and would sun themselves on the roofs of surrounding outbuildings, where their pompous strutting and homely cooing added greatly to the warmth and contentment of those long sleepy summer days. Later I was given a pair of these pigeons, and they lent an air of great distinction to the large and thriving flock of very ordinary birds that I had bred from the original pair I had acquired years before from Farmer Gorringe.

Inspired by Colonel Ismay, who overcame my earlier prejudices, I suddenly decided to join the army, but as I had not even taken the School Certificate I had to do something drastic about that first. I went to stay with the retired headmaster of a prep school at Bowness on Lake Windermere. Mr Snow had been headmaster at The Craig, a school at which his son-in-law had succeeded him as principal. After his retirement Mr Snow used to take occasional pupils for private tuition in subjects at which they were weak. I was hopeless at mathematics and on this subject I now concentrated. For the first time in my life I really worked. The house, Mylnbeck, stood beside the road that ran between Windermere and Bowness, a small lakeside town, which even in those days was a mecca for tourists. It was a grey stone building, which seemed somehow to have been quarried in one piece from the surrounding fells and stood divided by a small square of garden from the Beck, a shallow, fast-flowing stream of such clearness that I never hesitated to drink from it whenever I felt inclined. Mr Snow and his wife were a most kindly pair with a curiously Victorian air about them. Like many men of his profession he had a dry sense of humour, which amused me a great deal. He was extremely erudite and yet was able to make even the dullest subject seem interesting.

Although I had to devote a great deal of time to my books, there were yet many hours, particularly in the evening, when I was free to explore the district and to find out all I could about the inhabitants, human and otherwise. The Fell farmers, with their slow northern speech, kindliness and deep involvement with nature in all her moods, appealed to me enormously. I soon made myself at home in this lovely county; and to me West-morland still vies with Northumberland and Sussex in being one of my three favourite English counties. Not only is the scenery lovely, as the thousands of annual visitors would agree, but the people are a race apart, directly descended from the Vikings, who colonised this wild part of Britain. They not only look in many instances Scandinavian but have a number of curious words and phrases that have changed little, if at all, from the original Norse. 'Liaal,' meaning little or small, is a typical example. A friend of mine was attending a meet of the local fox hounds, accompanied by his elegant and aristocratic sheep-dog bitch, when he was rather disconcerted to overhear two old Westmorland farmers refer to his dog as 'a bonny liaal cur,' cur being the local name for any sheep-dog or collie.

It did not take long for me to find a lot in common with these men, whose interests were in so many cases similar to mine. Nearly every other house had a loft of racing pigeons, and this sport was followed very keenly indeed. Then there was Fell hound racing, a speciality of this part of the world. The hounds, which bore little resemblance to their neighbours of the Ullswater and other Fell packs of fox hounds, were long rangy beasts that could well have been the result of greyhound-pointer cross. They were not much to look at, being lightly boned almost to the point of weediness, but their owners prized them, and many of the Fell families had one or more of these unusual and distinctive dogs.

The method of racing was for a runner to lay an aniseed trail over fell and dale, a distance of ten miles or there-abouts, the finish being in the same field as the start. The hounds were slipped and shot away at fantastic speed, their high-pitched gull-like yelping getting fainter and fainter until it vanished amidst the brooding silence of the granite-scarred hills; soon, however, it could be heard afar as the hounds drew closer again until they could be seen white against the browns and greens of the fellside; and now their owners yelling like savage tribesmen would race for the finishing line, waving aniseed-soaked rags and shouting home their own particular pride and joy. The hounds, their stamina undiminished, would come pouring in like a dappled tide, each one to leap at the rag held by its owner, and to be swung high in the air to the sound of cheers and applause, mingled with the curses of unlucky punters. Considerable sums of money were staked on these events and skulduggery, I regret to say, was not unknown, cases having been recorded where certain villainous characters armed with fishing nets had lurked behind dry stone walls out of sight of spectators to nobble the favourites.

Sheep-dog Trials too were a very popular sport, and much less known in the south, with the exception of Wales, than is the case to-day. The majority of dogs owned by Westmorland sheep farms were the black-and-white border collies. So popular and clever were these dogs that they have now spread far beyond their land of origin to every country in the world where sheep are reared. Occasionally on some of the more remote farm-steads you would find a different breed of dog, the shaggy-coated bearded collie with its grey topknot and wistful expression. These were immortalised by Alfred Oliphant in *Owd Bob*, one of the best dog stories ever written.

I enjoyed these expeditions deep into the heart of Westmorland but, although I was never bored, I yearned at times for a companion to share such experiences with me. One day I was bicycling through the streets of Windermere when I saw loping towards me a great rough-haired iron-grey dog like a deerhound in a medieval tapestry. This was the dog for me. As this splendid animal drew level, I pulled up and called him; he half cocked his ears, grinned and bounded up, leering confi-dentially. He wore no collar but he seemed perfectly at ease and did not have the pathetic, furtive look of a stray;

he gave the impression of being much at home on his own territory. After a brief conversation he went on his way, turned down a side-street and on reaching a particular house reared on his hind legs against the door and thumped loudly with his forepaws, at the same time baying with a deep rich baritone. The door opened and the dog disappeared within.

On the spur of the moment I jumped off my bike, put it against a convenient wall, and knocked at the door behind which the dog had disappeared. It was opened by one Bernard Bracken, a colourful character of whom I had heard much, but had not hitherto had the pleasure of meeting. He asked me in, and I went straight to the point. Would he sell the dog? No, he would not; he would never part with this wonder dog at any price. Didn't Switch provide the whole family with food, and to spare? Wasn't he the fastest, cleverest, most loyal and bravest dog in the north? Oh no! To sell him would be unthinkable. However, he did just happen to have a friend, a partner in crime, who had a bitch, a little sister to this paragon, who might conceivably be induced to part with her, for a good price of course. It appeared that this other fellow, also a professional poacher, lived in Kendal in a street of uncommon ill repute. I had heard much about this particular street and the evil goings on there, but it would have taken much more than such rumours to keep me from the chance of possessing such a dog.

I arranged to meet Bernard Bracken and his friend in a hostelry in this seamy locality on the Saturday night. It was a Dickensian setting, the bar with its hunting scenes and cock-fighting pictures, the lights dim but diffused, reflecting from the pewter mugs on the shelves, the brasses and the old-fashioned gas fittings. The bar was crowded with men, most of whom wore spotted handkerchiefs around their necks and shapeless caps upon their heads. The roar of conversation faltered and ceased as I entered,

73

and at once the burly form of Bernard Bracken detached itself from a small group in the corner by the bar and beckoned me to join them. He ordered me a half-pint of light ale, and introduced me to his friends, whose appearance I did not even notice for I had eyes only for the dog, which lay beneath a wooden seat.

She was a lurcher bitch of the real old-fashioned sort, shaggy, russet brindled, with a white blaze and tail tip. Her jaws were heavily bearded and from beneath her grizzled, bushy eyebrows there shone a pair of lustrous brown eyes, honest, kindly and steadfast. A piece of twine was attached to her collar, and with this her owner pulled her from beneath her shelter. She came reluctantly, her tail half wagging, her eyes looking up shyly, as if to see what manner of man her new owner might be. I knelt to pat her head and she thrust her long gentle muzzle deep into my hands, and gazed at me with an expression in which hope and pleading were intermingled. She was almost nine months old and, although thin, was otherwise in fair condition. I asked his price and dreaded the answer, lest he named a figure beyond that which I carried in my pocket. He told me, 'Fifteen bob.' Fifteen shillings, and I was expecting that it would be at least a couple of pounds. I had that morning cashed a cheque for £5, all the money I owned in the world. I nearly choked with relief. I paid rapidly, bought the man a pint of beer, shook hands, and left the pub before he could change his mind.

The bitch trotted by my side at the end of her bedraggled bit of cord, her head and tail held low. I spoke to her, her tail waved gently and her eyes glanced up at me. I stopped to talk to her, to let her know that she was now my dog, and come what may we would share everything from that moment onwards. I had not asked her name, because I had already decided what to call her. With her colour, a warm golden reddish brown, shaded with a faint barring of dark wavy lines, her crisp wiry weather-resistant coat, together with the circumstances of our meeting, she could have only one name, and that name was Bracken. She was the first dog I had ever owned completely, Shifter being a family dog. She was one of the best dogs I have ever owned and the one whose characteristics still stand out most clearly of all. She came to me at my most impressionable age, and she was still with me nearly fifteen years later.

I regretted that I had not asked permission to keep a dog at Mylnbeck, but the whole thing had happened so speedily that I had not fully realised what the outcome would be. I made her a comfortable bed of straw in an outhouse and fed her well, perhaps the first really substantial meal she had had since she had left her mother. Seeing her comfortably settled I patted her, told her to behave herself and left her. I had hardly fallen asleep when it started. A long melancholy wolf-like howl, carrying all the depths of sorrow in her soul, broke into my consciousness. I slipped downstairs in dressing-gown and pyjamas, and spent the remainder of the night with her curled together in the straw.

Thus we lay until the first pale probings of dawn touched the enveloping blackness of the distant fells, bringing the storm cock to his song station in the great ash tree above the Beck. I hurried into trousers and pullover, flung open the door of the shed, and Bracken was free. We crossed the Beck by the great flat moss-covered stones where the loaches hid and out on to the sheep-grazed lower slopes of the fell side. Bracken stayed close beside me until the light strengthened and then left me, cantering into the far distance with the tireless stride I was to know so well; she would pause silhouetted atop of a stone wall, her head cocked for my whistle, then she came bounding back at once, clearing walls and gates with the ease of an experienced steeplechaser.

It was clear from the first that she now regarded herself as my dog, and that she was well content that it should be so. She never gave her full love to anyone else, not even

to my mother, who was devoted to her, and who looked
after her for many months when in wartime it was impossible for her to be with me. After our first walk
together I gave her some breakfast and a drink of milk
and returned her to her shed. I then confessed to Mr
Snow, who could not have been more understanding.
With that hurdle behind us the future looked bright.

With Bracken beside me I was inspired to travel
farther afield and together we would cross Lake Windermere by the ferry to visit 'Lancashire above the Sands,'
as attractive a corner of Lakeland as could be found in
either Cumberland or Westmorland. There was a particularly fascinating village called Hawkshead, inappropriately named as far as I was concerned, as I failed to
find even a kestrel in the area. There was, however, a
great precipice full of huge, loose boulders, from which
trees were growing and which was heavily wooded on all
sides. Here one afternoon Bracken put up some small
quarry from a thicket close to the path. She cleared a
great pile of dead wood and vanished into the surrounding
greenery. Soon I heard her giving tongue far ahead of
me, and scrambling and stumbling I came up with her,
to find her leaping against the trunk of a huge Scots pine.
Looking up I saw far above my head a flash of reddish
brown fur; a red squirrel? These were then quite common

in the area, the grey being unknown at that time. There was a sudden commotion in the branches and something big and dark hurtled across a gap and landed in the next tree, whilst Bracken became almost berserk with excitement. I stood close against the trunk of the tree and peered upwards; suddenly I saw a movement and I could make out a small, fierce triangular face with little upright ears and bright inquiring eyes. It was a pine marten, one of the rarest animals in Britain.

Calling Bracken to heel and soothing her, I sat on my rucksack and watched. For some minutes this most graceful of our mammals studied me from all angles and eventually, I assume, came to the conclusion that either we were harmless or else unable to climb. Suddenly it appeared to relax, sat up in the fork of a tree and started washing itself. Then, slowly, to my extreme excitement, it came down branch after branch, until I had one of the most perfect views of this delightful creature that it is possible to imagine. Picking up something in its mouth, casually and with wonderfully controlled ease it sprang from one tree to the next, while I watched it motionless, with Bracken now completely silent, though taking as much interest in this as her master.

Some fifty yards away there was a hole, obviously the deserted nest of a woodpecker. I had noticed this hole on previous occasions, but had not regarded it as having any special significance. A convenient branch sprouted from the trunk a foot or more above the hole; the pine marten reached this and lay stretched out as if resting, its tail hanging gracefully like a fox's brush to one side. The pine marten, which I now saw was carrying the body of some rodent, gave a series of queer chuckling grunts, not unlike those of an excited ferret. As I watched a tiny face appeared at the hole, and to my delight a beautiful pine marten kitten emerged and climbed to the branch beside its parent. It was followed by another and another, until there were three tiny pine martens on the branch.

The kittens, which were of a light creamy colour, not unlike that of a Siamese cat, except for their faces which resembled their parent's, grabbed the prey and a terrific game of tag followed. The youngsters showed themselves to be every whit as skilled tree climbers as their parent, and I was privileged to watch for a good five minutes a spectacle which is not given to many to witness. From far away came the echoing shot of a twelve-bore and where a second before there had been four pine martens not a trace was to be seen, the family had vanished deep into the interior of the tree. I kept this secret to myself, as these lovely animals, for all their harmlessness and rarity, are by no means safe from trigger-happy trophy hunters, and do not receive even the meagre protection awarded to the rarer birds.

Far out on a lonely plateau surrounded by great screes, whose granite outcrops somehow gave the impression of petrified waterfalls, was a small lake, School Knot Tarn. This lake, silent, black and forbidding when I visited it at dusk, seemed to have escaped from the pages of *Morte d'Arthur*. I would have been only mildly surprised to have seen an arm clothed in white samite rising from the depths brandishing the sword Excalibur. It was a mystic, haunted place, and I was glad to have the company of Bracken, who was not overawed by the atmosphere. However, as she was leaving the lake-side she suddenly growled quietly, raised her hackles and took a few steps forward. I looked in the direction she was indicating; fifty yards away, his grey tinged coat blending with the encroaching gloom, one paw raised, stood a big hill fox, larger, darker and longer legged than his cousin from the shires. The hill fox, also known as the greyhound fox, is quite distinct from the better-known red fox, although it is, of course, a local variation. He lives up to his local name and takes a deal of catching when once he has pointed his mask in the direction of the wild crags where he has his den.

Bracken was a real countryman's dog, of the type that has been the companion and working partner of poachers and gypsies from time immemorial; the kind of dog, of whom it could be said with little exaggeration, that you could put her in one end of a field or spinney and she would come out the other end with a dinner in her mouth. But above all, and this is imperative in a dog destined to live a full life in a farming district, she was rock steady with stock. I have known her on several occasions to course a hare through the middle of a flock of sheep without glancing to left or right. If she was working a field in which stock were grazing she would canter on with her long elastic stride around the perimeter, working inwards to the centre, her circles decreasing until she had covered the whole ground, whilst the sheep or cattle, somehow sensing her indifference, would hardly raise their heads. In my ignorance I assumed after this that all hunting dogs or hounds were naturally 'wedded' to their legitimate quarry and would ignore anything else. I found out just how wrong I was when later I took a Saluki for a day's hunting on the South Downs.

The only time Bracken let me down was when I took her for a walk in Richmond Park, and she took off after the first red deer she met, a magnificent stag, and coursed him. To catch her I had to scramble over one of the almost unclimbable park walls with a mounted ranger almost on our heels. I never took her there again. It was really my fault, because we had returned only a few days before from a visit to my uncle in Scotland where deer were legitimate quarry, though a lurcher of Bracken's size and weight would, of course, be entirely outmatched. Still, the chase was all that mattered to either of us.

She was completely obedient to call or whistle. I once relieved a sceptical old Lakeland farmer of five shillings when Bracken coursed a rabbit and caught it at least three fields away; he had been extolling the virtues of his sheep-dog which was indeed all that a well-trained collie should be. The farmer lost his bet that Bracken would not retrieve to hand. I was in some doubt myself at that time but was prepared to uphold her honour. I whistled, Bracken picked up her quarry, and clearing three stone walls *en route* laid the rabbit at my feet. A field trial champion could not have done better. She later did this on several occasions and I was very proud of her.

She was a splendid bitch to look at too; twenty-four inches to the shoulder, with the glamour of a deerhound with her unusual red golden colour, and wavy black stripes. She was the daughter of a deerhound/greyhound father and a greyhound/Bedlington mother; she had the Roman nose of the Bedlington and rat-trap jaws, but she showed very little of the quick temper and aggressiveness common to the terrier breeds. She could on occasion fight with the best of them and had a well-developed instinct for the protection of my person and property, but was basically a gentle, self-effacing dog with impeccable manners. I may seem over-generous with praise, but she was my first dog and twenty years after her death I still feel it behoves me to pay tribute to the years of happiness and companionship that she gave me.

A few weeks after I became the owner of Bracken I went home for a month's holiday. I had bought a collar and lead for her. The collar was a splendid affair, a broad band of deep red leather with an intricate pattern of scrolls and squiggles, formed by inlaid metal beautifully worked into the leather. It was the work of a craftsman, such as is seldom seen to-day. He had a little shop in a back street in Kendal. Although to the best of my knowledge she had never travelled by train, Bracken behaved superbly, curled into a tight coil somehow resembling an oversized Chelsea bun with a dog's face sticking out of it. She was completely unawed by the crowds and traffic of London, and accepted the pats and fuss made by admiring strangers. There was something about her, an air of having stepped out of an earlier age which, together with her gentle dignity, attracted a great deal of attention wherever she went.

My mother drove us down to Old Acres and was immediately won over by her, and remained her devoted friend from then on. Shifter was at first rather grumpy, but then he was fourteen years old, and had always been cock of the walk. However, even he was soon on the best of terms and he seemed to acquire a new lease of life when he went diving into thickets to drive out the expected rabbits for Bracken to catch. I was amused at the reaction of the countryman to this most countryish of country dogs. The policemen looked at her askance and I feel sure made a mental note to keep an eye on the pair of us. The farmers were interested from a sporting point of view and gave me permission to take her over their land to keep the rabbits down. But the local poaching fraternity were soon on my doorstep with offers to buy her, which needless to say I indignantly refused.

Two of her most devoted admirers, apart from her own immediate family circle, were my two cousins, Spearman Swinburne and Ida Stewart (also born a Swinburne). Spearman was then a busy G.P. at Hawkhurst, in Kent. He was an enthusiastic naturalist and dog man, with a taste for the unusual. He owned what he proudly described as a lurcher, which was, in fact, more like a small drover's dog; but Bob was a great character and fast enough to turn a hare. He had a ridiculous stump of a tail, a shortcoming of which he seemed acutely and embarrassingly aware. Spearman was a very clever doctor, but at heart I think he would have preferred to be a vet. In fact, he once confided to me how much he regretted that his life was devoted to the only really unattractive animals in the world.

Cousin Ida was a formidable figure, the terror of anyone whom she even suspected of being unkind to animals. She was immensely tall and strong, with a courage and personality to match. She would march up to any house where she saw a dog chained to a kennel and demand to see the owner. After telling the dog owner exactly what she thought of him she would thrust what she considered to be the value of the dog into his hands and depart with the erstwhile captive trotting beside her. The result of this benevolent 'dog napping' was that her house was often crammed to bursting with dogs of all kinds, and all with splendid names in no way influenced by their very ordinary antecedents. There was Fernworthy, named after the village in Devon from which he had been rescued; he once had an appalling fight with Shifter, when the two who had been happily rabbiting all the afternoon were leashed together to cross the main road. There was also Miss Jones, a lugubrious half Labrador from Wales; and The White Earl of Whitford, known to his intimates as William Wazik, a small white terrier-like dog with possibly a dash of dachshund in his ancestry. Wandering alone late at night on a dangerous thoroughfare, he had been picked up by Cousin Ida who had, of course, overlooked the formality of seeking his legal owner or even informing the police. She seldom went anywhere unless accompanied by some of her retinue. I remember on one of her visits, when I brought her an early morning cup of tea, I was amazed and delighted to see Cousin Ida fast asleep, with Fernworthy's head on one side of the pillow and Miss Jones on the other, all blissfully happy.

Cousin Ida was an antagonist to be reckoned with. Once in Newcastle she noticed a rag and bone man belabouring a heavily overloaded pony. She leaped out of the bus and set about the fellow with her umbrella, and he was rash enough to retaliate with his whip. It must have been quite a battle while it lasted. Needless to say she emerged triumphant if slightly breathless; what happened to the owner of the pony history does not relate, but doubtless he survived. The man who described the wounded buffalo as the world's most dangerous animal could not have encountered Cousin Ida on the rampage. Luckily for me we always got along splendidly and spent many happy hours together, bird-watching, butterfly-spotting and dog-walking. I remember we once enlivened a rather dreary London dinner-party given by my grand-mother by our own individual renderings of the mating call of the dabchick. It was Cousin Ida who persuaded me to keep a nature diary, a practice I continued for many years. She was also responsible for my joining the British Empire Naturalists' Association, a splendid organ-isation which I fear must have been disbanded or else become affiliated with some other body.

Chapter 7

In the fullness of time I acquired a commission in the Supplementary Reserve of the Green Howards. I did a few months' training in the spring of 1939 at the depot at Richmond, in Yorkshire, and I thoroughly enjoyed my time there. I took Bracken with me, and she was a great success, adding variety to the more usual springers and Labradors owned by many of the regular officers. The sudden transformation from a not particularly successful schoolboy to being a member of an Officers' Mess was a curious experience. After all, I had not been to

Sandhurst and I was still only eighteen years old. In fact, it took me some time to get used to being accepted in adult company at all, and the fact that anyone should actually ask my advice on any subject was a matter to amaze me.

The depot was staffed by regular officers who were either waiting to be posted to one of the battalions, or had been attending some course or other such as the Small Arms School at Hythe, or, having completed home leave, were filling in time before returning to the 1st Battalion in Palestine. These officers' duties were to train newly enlisted recruits or to instruct people like myself how to behave as a future regular officer. The idea, so far as I was concerned, was that I should spend a couple of months at the depot, learning such things as Arms Drill, the use of the bren gun, simple Tactical Exercises without Troops, and so on. I would then join the 1st Battalion, which was due to return from overseas service in August. There I would go on manœuvres and learn how to command an infantry platoon. After a month or so, provided I passed the exam and acquitted myself to the satisfaction of my superiors, I would become one of that select fellowship of happy warriors, a Regular Army 2nd Lieutenant.

I finished my course more or less successfully; at least I was not drummed out. I even received quite an encouraging report from the C.O. and the other officers, who had worked hard and painstakingly to give me some semblance of a potential regular officer. I left the depot with orders to report to the 1st Battalion in August, when it returned from overseas. I had three months to fill in somehow.

Major Charlie Kirkwood was a former brother officer of my father. They had served together in the Indian campaigns. Charlie had been captured by the Turks and had spent some years in captivity in appalling conditions, but this had in no way destroyed his ebullience or zest for life. He was an Irishman and he lived with his wife, Ivy, and two daughters at St John's Wood when he was not at his ancestral home at Woodbrooke in County Roscommon. Their home was always filled with people and life seemed to be one long glorious party. Charlie was a natural horseman, and an artist of great enthusiasm if limited talent. Ivy had trained as an opera singer and had one of the most fascinating speaking voices I have ever heard. She was also an extremely attractive woman and a natural hostess. Antoinette, the younger daughter, known as Tony, was at that time training to be a ballet dancer, and was a violinist of no mean ability. She was also a keen horsewoman and we enjoyed many splendid rides together, accompanied by two little Welsh sheep-dogs called Sian and Trimmer, and it was to this happy, lively household that Bracken and I descended in July 1939.

We had been invited to St John's Wood before travelling *en famille* to Ireland, where I was to stay until joining the battalion in August. In London we spent our time visiting museums and the zoo, and exercising our dogs in Richmond Park and Hampstead Heath where, incidentally, the dogs put up and coursed a dog fox, which had been helping itself from a litter basket within half a mile of The Spaniards' Inn. Thus the days passed until the day came to cross the Irish Sea.

It was quite an invasion force: five adults, two children and three dogs, and two other families of London friends who joined us at the station. We travelled by train to Holyhead and took the Irish packet to Dun Laoghaire. Of the crossing I will say little. The Irish Sea was in a particularly savage mood; I found a convenient space on deck and remained there with Bracken pressed against me for comfort and warmth in a state of semi-coma until we reached Ireland. Even after leaving the ship I took some time to get back to normal. I thought back with little regret to the time that I had declined Kurt Hahn's suggestion that I should join the Merchant Navy.

Bracken, on the other hand, had not suffered at all. We still had several hours' journey before us, and a considerable wait for the train, which like most things in Ireland was individual in its ways and obeyed few laws of God or man. Still feeling a bit groggy and saying that Bracken must stretch her legs after the discomfort of the crossing, I made my excuses and arranged to meet the rest of the party at the station.

Dun Laoghaire, apart from the harbour which is magnificent, did not strike me as an attractive town. I wandered off down some rather seedy back streets looking for a public garden or at least a plot of grass where Bracken could obey the long-delayed calls of nature. We must have been longer and going farther than I realised, and I was about to start back when a motor car of a sort drew up beside me. It was an ancient affair, with an open roof, and I soon noticed with relief that it was intended for a taxi. The driver leaned out and, peering at Bracken, 'Can she catch hares?' he asked. I assured him that she most certainly could catch hares. 'Well,' said he, and I make no effort to emulate his manner of speaking, 'well, we have a hare in our field as big as a pony, and I'm thinking he'd have the legs of that dog!' I assumed that this was some sort of challenge. I told him that I had a train to catch, but that at any other time I would have taken him up on it. I would anyway be hard put to catch the train. Could he take me to the station? 'Jump in, sor,' says he, 'I'll have you there in a jiffy.' Bracken and I settled in the back seat, which like the car had seen better days, and we lurched off. I paid little attention to where we were going and more to keeping myself and the dog from falling off the seat. The car jerked to a stop and I opened the door expecting to see the station. The driver was crouched over the wheel with his head in his hands, and we were back where we had started from. I asked him what the devil he thought he was doing. 'I'm sorry, sor,' says he, 'but it's drunk I am, as drunk as a pig, but

I'll not be chargin' you for it.' Finally I had to leap out and ask a passing native the way to the station, and with me bellowing instructions in his ear we roared off once again. To my intense relief we did arrive just in time. True to his word the man flatly refused to take a penny, but begged me to come back one day to meet those hares of his, a date I have unfortunately never been able to keep. Eventually the train did get under way and we rumbled across the lovely plains of Ireland.

Woodbrooke, the Kirkwoods' home, was all that one might expect such an establishment to be. The house, a large grey stone building, looked out on one side to the stable-yard and all the whitewashed outbuildings associated with it, and on the other to a terraced garden, beyond which field after yellow-green field, rushy and tussocky, the haunt of hare and stoat, stretched away towards the blue-grey misty hills. The River Shannon broadened out into a lake on one side, where lived a gaggle of domestic geese, which were as shy as their wild cousins of the Scottish lakes and moorlands. The lake was swarming with perch of all sizes, singularly unsophisticated as one had only to drop a baited hook over the side of the waterlogged old rowing-boat, which jutted out from the side of the bank and served as a jetty, to catch as many fish as one wanted.

The Home Farm was run by a family called Maxwell; there appeared to be a prodigious number of brothers, of whom I can remember only two, Willie and Johnnie. They were a wild bunch, and keen sportsmen to a man. In no time at all they had organised hunting meetings, attended by what appeared to be the entire male population of the district. The Irish hare has long held a reputation for speed, cunning and stamina, although he is but a subspecies of the ordinary European hare. With Bracken on its scut it needed all this and more. It seemed that most Irishmen owned at least one greyhound, and the plains of Boyle was the Saturday evening venue of most of these excellent gentlemen. One old fellow, an acknowledged authority on all aspects of field sports, after seeing Bracken in action told me quite spontaneously and with little of the usual Irish flair for flattery and exaggeration that he had never seen a dog get on terms with a hare as quickly as she did. Later she ran against a well-known winner from the Mullingar Track, where many a good performer at the White City and Wembley have made their débuts. She was beaten after a gruelling run, but made enough impression to earn the name of 'The Flying Brindle,' which pleased me enormously.

Willie Maxwell had his own peculiar sense of humour. Noticing a fine crop of mushrooms in a field where a herd of cattle and a particularly truculent-looking bull were grazing, I asked whether the bull was savage. 'It is not,' he assured me. 'We have no wicked cattle here.' Relieved to hear this, I climbed the gate forthwith and was soon busy amongst the mushrooms, some of which were nearly as big as saucers. I kept a wary eye on the bull which was extremely large and black and looked like a refugee from a Spanish arena. However, it appeared to be intent on grazing and was paying no attention to me. I was right out in the middle of the field and had taken off my coat to put the mushrooms in. This was nearly full and I was just about to pick it up and withdraw when I heard a snort that would not have disgraced a rhino. Horrified, I turned round to see the bull, his tail stuck up like a poker, his head about on a level with my midriff, coming after me like a racehorse, the earth resounding with the thundering of his hooves. I would not have thought it possible that anything so ponderous could move so fast. I did my best ever time for the sprint and reached the gate barely a horn's length ahead of my pursuer who, balked of his prey, trotted back to his admiring herd and continued grazing as if nothing had happened. When I had recovered a modicum of self-control I turned to Willie who appeared helpless with merriment. I demanded an explanation. 'Sure, sor,' said he, 'the crature must have guessed you were a Protestant.' I suggested that he should retrieve my mushrooms, which he did, and the bull never so much as glanced at him.

The Kirkwoods had amongst their hunters and children's ponies an ancient cart mare called Molly. She was said to be about thirty years old, but like Cleopatra, age could not wither her nor curb her gallant spirit. She was big, about sixteen hands, with a back as broad as a hippopotamus. She was the complete all-rounder; she would pull a light cart to the village for the week's shopping, she helped with the roller, and she was the perfect beginner's mount. She would canter and trot for miles, was capable of a surprisingly speedy gallop for a short distance and could jump any reasonable obstacle; those she could not manage she would bulldoze through like a buffalo. She had the most kindly and gentle temperament; if I came unstuck, which was often, she would glide quietly to a halt and wait to be remounted, and not hightail it for home as fast as she could as did most of her more aristocratic stable mates. She had, amongst other virtues, a strongly developed homing instinct, and if, as frequently happened, she and I and Bracken were overtaken by darkness on one of our crepuscular expeditions far into the surrounding countryside, Molly could be depended upon to bring us safely to port again.

I enjoyed my stay in Ireland. I liked the informality, the friendliness and welcome one received on many an unannounced visit to one of the several large demesnes. As in all country districts at this time, everyone knew everyone else, and people had time to be themselves and were not hounded by the demons of worry and endless, pointless rushing about and the eternal feeling of being on the brink of a precipice, which seems to be almost universal to-day. For me, however, there was one curious quality about Ireland which I have never noticed elsewhere. I can only describe it as a sort of over-excitement mixed with melancholy. I have never heard anyone else mention this, nor have I read about it, so I can only conclude that it was something personal, and may have been something to do with my emotional development at that time. Anyway, it was a feeling very peculiar and not altogether unpleasant, but it disappeared for ever as soon as I set foot on the boat for home.

The 1st Battalion the Green Howards were due at Catterick and I was to join them. Bracken and I were alone at Dun Laoghaire for the return journey to Holyhead; once more I had time to spare, once more I prowled the streets. Ireland had not quite finished her puckish tricks on me yet. Rounding a corner I came across a tinker character with a large she-ass across whose back was slung a basket full of vegetables. By her side trotted a half-grown foal. If there is one thing that I cannot resist it is a donkey foal. If there is a more attractive animal in the world I have yet to meet it, with its chubby face, offset with enormous ears which seem completely out of proportion, its woolly body and tiny wagging tail, the whole supported by ridiculously long legs, which seem hardly under the owner's complete control, and its expression, half shy yet full of humour. The owner rightly sensing the presence of a sucker inquired slyly:

'Would you be wanting a young ass, sor?' It appears the word donkey is out of general use to the west of the Irish Sea.

'How much?' I asked.

'Twenty-five shillings, y'r honour!' said he.

'Done,' said I, having no idea of the value of these beasts of burden, but this seemed too good to miss. He produced a halter out of his pocket and slipped it on. I started on our way to the docks, little realising what a journey I had let myself in for. The foal was quite content to stay in Ireland; he bucked and reared and waltzed like a professional dancer in all directions but the right one. In despair I grabbed the halter by the cheek strap

and put all my weight into the struggle, and we started on our way. Receiving some pretty black looks and obscene language from the motor cars encountered on the route, we made slow progress, with Bracken prancing round in circles barking loudly, as if to announce our coming to those who were not already aware of it. However, determination finally prevailed.

I reached the gangway of the boat and looked about us. What I was going to do with my new acquisition had not entered very seriously into my consideration. Should I present myself at Battalion Headquarters in full uniform, riding on this fiery steed? I saw a seaman doing something nautical to a rope, so hailed him and asked if there was room on the vessel for one small donkey, accompanied by its owner and its owner's dog. The seaman took one look at this spectacle and raced aboard, returning shortly with a gentleman covered with gold rings. I repeated my request. 'Could I possibly take my donkey aboard, at my own risk, of course?' 'No, ye cannot, ye cannot take your ass with ye,' he thundered. So that was that. Sadly I returned to the spot where I had tethered my ass to a bollard, and found a nice, quiet old man, obviously understanding how to treat such beasts. 'I'll give you £2 for the ass,' said he. So ended my experiences in the realm of donkey ownership.

I arrived back at Eaton Place in London, after a much better crossing than the last one, but still took a few days to get back to normal after the heady and vaguely unreal atmosphere of Ireland. My mother was spending a week or so there after one of her expeditions to the Continent. At that time there was a lot of talk of Adolf Hitler and his intentions, and the name Danzig had a habit of cropping up.

I joined the 1st Battalion at Catterick and was soon involved body and soul in what at that time I believed was to become my life's work. The battalion was commanded by Lt.-Colonel Robinson, and the officers were the usual ex-Sandhurst types that one would expect to find in a regular infantry battalion. I met one or two old acquaintances from the depot, and soon made friends with the other subalterns, most of whom were a decent crowd. Whatever they may have felt, they showed no contempt for the stranger, a mere supplementary reservist in their midst. I was lucky as the company to which I was attached was commanded by the nephew of an old friend of my father. He was a keen sportsman and had a trio of exceedingly hard-bitten working terriers. His wife, who was living with him in married quarters nearby, had been joint master of a smart and dashing pack of Irish foxhounds, so we had a lot in common.

Bracken once more proved her worth as a great ice-breaker and she and I and many others had a lot of sport on the windy heather-clad Yorkshire moors. Soon the battalion moved to camp for manœuvres. For the first time Bracken and I were separated. She had to stay behind. I was now in charge of an infantry platoon, all the members of which were experienced. I always found it vaguely embarrassing having to give orders to men who had obviously forgotten more than I was ever likely to learn. However, I had a very good platoon sergeant-major who helped me along and prevented me from making too much of an ass of myself; the other N.C.O.s were also most understanding and put up with my short-comings and taught me a great deal.

In time I might have become a reasonably efficient offcer. This, however, was not to be. The crisis deepened, Britain delivered her ultimatum and Hitler invaded Poland. The battalion hurried to Catterick to await the outcome. My mother came up to spend the weekend; she and I and Bracken were all together in the lounge of the King's Head Hotel at Richmond when we heard Neville Chamberlain announce that we were at war with Germany. The long-expected climax had come. This was it. What now? The sirens went and Britain awaited annihilation; the whole might of the Luftwaffe must be on its way to pulverise us. The all-clear went and Britain breathed again.

Chapter 8

I HAD to report back to Battalion Headquarters to see what fate had in store for me. My mother and I decided that she would take Bracken back to Old Acres, as it was possible that I might be posted overseas immediately. For days the battalion waited with growing impatience. Now that we were committed we wanted to get on with it, get it over and get back to our accustomed way of life. A few days later we had orders to parade in full marching order for inspection by the Area Commander. I took my place at the head of my platoon, the C.O. appeared and the band struck up the Regimental March, the 'Bonny Yorkshire Rose,' one of the most haunting of all martial airs. We marched past the saluting base, column after column, and then reformed to hear the General's words. The battalion was leaving at once for 'somewhere over there.' Well, we were all in it together and I could not wish for better comrades. I marched my platoon away and dismissed my men.

I was returning to the mess when I met an orderly room sergeant; I was to report to the adjutant at once. What he had to say made me feel numb with disappointment. I was too young and inexperienced to go overseas and was to report back to the depot for further training. I felt sick inside, a feeling that the commiseration of fellow subalterns did little to alleviate. I stood at the window of my room and watched the battalion march out to war. Six months later they were cut to pieces in Norway. Back at the depot I tried hard to interest myself in my duties and training, fully realising that I was as much in need of this as any of those under my command. To keep me occupied and to see that I earned my pay they sent me on various courses. This was fine in itself, but it wasn't getting me very far. I had joined the Supplementary Reserve at eighteen because I could think of nothing better to do with my life at that time, and I knew that I could always resign my commission and be something else. Now that the war had actually started, I wanted to be taking an active part; my ideas were a bit mixed up, but I was growing more and more discontented with the life I was leading.

I went up to London on leave, visited night clubs and danced at the Café de Paris. I went to the cinema and saw films such as *The Lion has Wings*, which made me more and more anxious to go and see the real thing and get on with the war. I never for a moment thought that those out there in the cold, the danger and discomfort, might well have sold their souls to change places with me.

One day I had lunch with 'Pug' Ismay, now a major-general and soon to rise higher still. It was a good lunch, the best his club could provide. I told him the whole story and he was sympathetic. I told him, amongst other things, that I felt inadequate and that I did not think I was sufficiently mature or experienced to take responsibility for the lives of other men in battle. I told him that I would like to resign my commission and join the ranks, and that if later I felt that I was worthy of it I would apply to go to an O.C.T.U. and start all over again. He did not explode, nor did he hold up my father's career as an example, but said little except that he understood how I felt. I realised, of course, that in wartime an officer could not resign his commission; it is not as simple as that. After my lunch I felt a great deal better, and returned to the depot and carried on as before. Most of my fellow officers were subalterns of 1914–18 vintage, none of whom can have been much under fifty. I remember they spent most of their spare time sitting about the mess drinking port or gin and grumbling about promotion or the lack of it. To me they were not an inspiring bunch.

One day the adjutant, another First World War hero, sent for me and told me that I was to go on indefinite leave pending the resignation of my commission. Although I cannot confirm it, I suspect that 'Pug' Ismay had taken my words to heart and used his influence on my behalf. I returned to Old Acres, and to Bracken, who was then being looked after by Grandmother and Nanny Hill, both of them having become very fond of her. It was a great life while it lasted. I was at home, I was getting full pay, and I was entitled to wear all the panoply of an officer's uniform. Later the rumour got around that I was doing something extremely hush-hush, though what this might be or why I should be doing it at home seems never to have been considered. I enjoyed this aura of mystery as I walked to the village on the most innocent of messages, and I could almost feel the cloak flowing from my shoulders and the dagger and hilt protruding from my gas-mask case.

All good things must come to an end. I received a telegram demanding my immediate presence at the depot.

I caught a train at once and thundered northward, feeling ready for anything that fate had to offer. The whole thing was brief and formal. In ten days I would be an ex-officer, a civilian: what I had wished for had come to pass. I was, however, still entitled to a first-class railway warrant, and I made sure I got it. I spent that night at the King's Head, and next day caught the train for London. A few days later I got a letter from my old school-fellow, Basil Chambers. He had enlisted in the Sherwood Foresters, a regiment of which his father had at one time been commanding officer.

Ten days later I presented myself to a recruiting sergeant in Brighton, received a railway warrant, 3rd class, and orders to proceed to Derby, at once if not sooner. I reported to Normanton Barracks, the regimental depot in Derby, where I received two suits of battle-dress, canvas leggings, great coat, rifle, etc. and all the rest of the grisly assortment that accompanied a private soldier and was supposed to constitute his whole world. I was now 49854193 Pte Summers of the 4th Regiment of Foot, the illustrious and greatly honoured Sherwood Foresters.

Staggering under my kitbag full of clobber, and with my rifle slung over my shoulder, I climbed into a fifteen-hundredweight truck which was to take me and a crowd of rather unhappy-looking fellow recruits to Eggington Hall, a requisitioned mansion between Derby and Burton-on-Trent. On arrival the truck slithered to a halt: feeling sick and decidedly subdued, we were received by a sergeant and somehow shepherded into three ranks. A corporal appeared and the two N.C.O.s barked orders, which nobody but myself understood. We trooped and stumbled off into the darkness towards the lowering pile that was to be our home during our initial training. We were shown into a room which was full of three-tier bunks. I threw my gear on to one of the lowest, sat on it and took stock of the situation. Hardly had I taken in my immediate surroundings than there was a bellow of recognition, Basil. I felt much as John Geste must have felt on being reunited with Beau at Sidi bel Abas. At the sight of Basil's cheerful and familiar features life, which had begun to look a trifle stark, became at least bearable.

We had hardly exchanged news before a bugle brayed outside and we had to troop out to the dining-hall for my first experience of army food and army tea as seen from the ranks. As an orderly officer I had had, as part of my duty, to inspect the men's dining-halls and listen to any complaints, and even to sample the food itself, but the thought that I might have actually to exist on it had never entered my head. Tea, I remember, consisted of doorsteps of bread and great slabs of cheese. The beverage was cocoa of unbelievable strength and not oversweetened either. That night as I lay in my bunk, cold, uncomfortable and hungry, listening to the blasphemies of my future comrades, I began to wonder if I had been so clever after all.

Basil was in another platoon and billeted on another floor, so I did not see much of him after that first night. Here at Eggington Hall we were put through our paces with great speed and efficiency. I knew about arms drill, could handle a rifle and bren gun, and was very fit, and that was about all that was required of a private. It was strange to me at first to be on the receiving end of orders and abuse from our N.C.O.s and to have to salute subalterns with whom I would formerly have been drinking in the mess. But I soon adapted myself and got used to it all. I must admit that one of the things I found hardest to accept was the foul-mouthed profanity of most of my comrades. It struck me as almost unbelievable that human beings should have so little power of self-expression. After a time, however, one became not only indifferent to such language but was apt to resort to it oneself without a second thought. I soon settled down to all the petty restrictions, peculiar discipline, annoyances and general 'bull' of army life as experienced in the ranks.

Our basic training soon came to an end; we were then considered to be fully trained soldiers ready to join a battalion of the line. Meanwhile the phony war had come to an end. Norway had been invaded, the Germans had overrun France, Belgium and Holland, and the evacuation from Dunkirk had been accomplished. We now awaited our turn, which we had no reason to believe would be long delayed. The Battle of Britain was fought and won, and London was rocking under the nightly assaults of the Luftwaffe. I was posted to the 2nd/5th Battalion at Folkestone early in the spring of 1942. Here life was much as usual: we went on route marches, we did P.T., and we dodged the minefields to swim in the chilly grey English Channel; we took part in all sorts of tactical exercises with our troops playing the part of the enemy. The French Canadians took this a bit too literally and used live ammunition, causing quite a few casualties, which did little to further Anglo-Canadian relations. We marched all over the south of England at record speed. We moved to Camber Sands beside the lovely medieval town of Rye, once a thriving port but now deserted by the sea. Behind the town the low-lying dyke-divided marshlands were the haunt of redshank, oyster-catcher and shoveller, and were grazed by the great red Sussex cattle and the Romney Marsh sheep with their curious spongy water-resisting hooves. Away towards the sea rose the remains of a Martello tower, once a bastion of defence against the might of Bonaparte, but now crumbling and ivy-shrouded; it had long been the home of a pair of kestrels, the little windhover, the russet-winged falcon of the Marshes.

This was, by and large, a happy period in my life. I was busy doing a worthwhile job, and part of a closely welded team, which had been brought together in some instances rather reluctantly but had now, after the rough edges had been smoothed down, become if not one great happy family at least a band of men united by a common cause. We shared our work, we slept as close as a pack of foxhounds, and in many cases we spent our spare time together.

The men in my platoon were mixed, but on the whole a most amiable crowd. There was Sergeant Coxon, a waggish fellow, who used to tell us long and involved stories of his experiences when on guard duty at Buckingham Palace; there was Corporal Boulton who was killed by a mortar shell during training and before he saw action; there was Lance-Corporal Stone from Somerset, who had fought his way out of Norway during that ill-fated expedition; there was Private Carver, known to his mates as Carver Doone; then there were the two inseparables, Privates Messam and Pinnock; and my own particular friend, Private Chollerton, a Derbyshire man of French extraction.

I was particularly lucky because my home at Horam was within easy cycling distance of the coast guard cottages where we were billeted. Furthermore, I soon found out that, provided I presented myself on parade on time and did not duck church parade or my stint on guard, I could do more or less what I liked. The discipline was there all right, but so long as we did not abuse it, it was not oppressive. I recall one morning when I was returning to billets after a weekend at home, for which I had not received an official pass. I did not, as caution should have dictated, avoid the township of Rye and take a more circuituous route. As luck would have it, just as I drew level with the main entrance of the largest and best hotel, The George, my Company Commander emerged, after no doubt an equally enjoyable though official escape from the rigours of warfare. Unfortunately he saw me, so making the best of a bad job I drew up and saluted as smartly as I could astride my machine. The O.C. smiled and wished me a good morning, and I heard no more of the incident.

I decided whilst on an official seventy-two hours' leave that it was time Bracken rejoined me. I had already made tentative inquiries about the reception she was likely to get, and when I thought the time was right I cycled back to Camber with her loping beside the bike. Bracken had, like Shifter, often followed me on expeditions and no distance appeared to be too great for her. She would canter beside me for ten or fifteen miles, hunt hard all day and return in the gloaming, with tail carried high and showing her contentment with the world. She was as hard and as fit as a timber wolf. She was welcomed in the billet, and though not officially on the strength was soon as well known in camp and on parade as she had been at home and in an officers' mess. She used to come with us on route marches and even on some localised schemes, and seldom failed to earn her keep. In those days a rabbit or hare was an uncommonly welcome addition to our frugal diet and our platoon must have been one of the best fed in the British Army. Her expertise was such that she soon earned the appellation Wonder Dog. This was fair enough, but as her reputation spread I had to keep a wary eye on her because it was by no means unknown for a dog to be enticed away or even stolen by neighbouring and dogless units.

We were officially on Coastal Defence, but we knew well enough that the gruelling training we were receiving was eventually to be used in a somewhat more aggressive role. The Dieppe Raid had come and gone, the Canadian Army had had its first baptism of fire, had suffered heavily and had proved its worth. Summer passed and our training intensified. We marched and counter-marched; we took part in all sorts of realistic assault courses in which live ammunition was fired a few inches over our heads; we learned to endure considerable hardship, to exist on a minimum of food, and to keep going when our minds and bodies cried out for food and sleep. However, we got used to it, and in fact we even began to enjoy it. The general who had thought all this up and applied it with remarkable success was not so well known then as he was later to become. His name was Bernard Montgomery.

With the autumn came the gales, and the marshes were blasted by icy winds and lashing rain that might well have come unabated from the wastes of Siberia. Then an incident occurred that must have influenced my whole way of life and enhanced my already intense feeling of unity with all kinds of furred and feathered beings. Training had finished for the day, the winds had dropped, and the evening sun glimmered over the marshes. High over head scattered groups of herring and blackheaded gulls drifted in from the direction of Dungeness, farther eastwards along the coast. I wanted for once to get away from the enforced companionship of the billet. I called Bracken and set off across the sand-dunes which, with their harsh wiry tufts of marram grass, looked like a miniature Sahara. Bracken, as ever, raced ahead of me, appearing as she topped the dunes almost a part of the setting, a creature of the wild places. She plunged out of sight behind a concrete pillbox and I followed hard on her heels. I lost sight of her and then I heard her barking. Bracken was a dog who seldom gave tongue without real cause, her very nature and her earliest training, when bound on some mysterious nocturnal business, forbade it. When I caught up with her I found she was cautiously examining some object that lay still half hidden in a hollow of a sand-dune. I quickly joined Bracken and knelt beside her; there, her blue-black eyes glaring fear and defiance, her hooked beak open in threat, and one wing trailing limply beside her, was a little female kestrel.

As I moved to pick her up, quick as light she flung herself on her back and grabbed my hand with needle-sharp claws; with her convulsive clutches they pene-

trated deep, and the pain inflicted was surprising considering how small and slight was my assailant. The little experience I had with hawks stood me in good stead at this moment. I took her in my right hand, holding her in a natural position, and waited for her to relax her grip, which she did after about half a minute. I then moved my left hand forward and upwards and, after gently detaching her claws, was able to hold her comfortably. I held out the injured wing; it did not appear to be broken, but I was not too happy about it. She was painfully emaciated, her breast-bone sharp as a paper-knife, and she felt as I held her as slight and frail as a handful of tissue paper. However, with her fighting spirit and, I hoped, the will to live, she had at least a chance.

What was I to do with her? One thing was certain; she couldn't be left where she was, to the mercy of the chill autumn night, and a prey to the first fox or black-backed gull that passed that way. But how did she come to be there in the first place? I could only suppose that, scouring the marshes in her search for field voles, she must have been swept by the recent gale into a telegraph wire and carried by the force of the wind and her own impetus to the hollow, and there had been slowly starving, maybe for several days. With little thought for what was to follow, I tucked her up inside my battle-dress tunic; then, calling Bracken, who had been a keen observer of what was to prove a momentous meeting, I returned hurriedly to my billet.

Chapter 9

THE reactions of my comrades on being introduced to the kestrel varied from expressions of outright blasphemy via open-mouthed astonishment to a genuine and sympathetic interest. It was plain that if she was to survive that night she would have to be fed, and quickly too. I asked the cook sergeant, who had often helped me with rations for Bracken, for a piece of raw meat, and he produced nearly enough to feed a condor, for which I blessed him. I put a towel across my knees and picked up the bird which I had installed in a basket, lined with newspaper, fixed to the carrier of my bicycle. I held her in my right hand with her wings and tail in as comfortable a position as possible, and her creamy black-streaked breast resting on the towel. She made little resistance, and with my left hand I managed to prise her mandibles apart and slip a small piece of meat over her tongue down the back of her throat. When her beak was released she gave a gulp and the meat had gone. I gave her several more pieces until I could feel that her crop had become slightly distended. I resisted the temptation to cram her to bursting point, put her back in her basket and left her in peace. An hour or so later I looked at her again. She seemed much more cheerful; she was standing up in a corner of the basket, her crop felt nearly empty, and I could see by the state of her droppings, or 'mutes,' that she had no internal injuries as I had feared.

Now it so happened that a few weeks earlier I had met in a local tavern a corporal in the R.A.M.C. John Sheldon had been a medical student who, at the outbreak of the war, had been about to take his finals but, being of an adventurous and even pugilistic temperament, had decided that medicine must wait and that his immediate interests lay in meeting the foe. He volunteered for an infantry regiment, but when the powers-that-be discovered his natural talents lay elsewhere he was transferred to the Medical Corps, where he was now a medical orderly or something similar.

That evening after supper I took the kestrel and went in search of John. I knew exactly in which bar to find him, so little time was lost. On hearing my story, and meeting his future patient, his whole attitude changed and he became at once the enthusiastic professional. He took me to his headquarters, where it seemed he had free access to any amount of medical paraphernalia. He looked at the injured wing and decided it was fractured but not badly. In no time at all he had made a most professional-looking splint, the bone was set and the two wings joined together and supported by a clever arrangement which passed right round the bird's body below the crop.

That night I lay sleepless thinking of my new acquisition, and above all what to call her, for it seemed that she would be with me for some weeks at least. I remembered a rumbustious book I had read as a boy, *Sir Devil May Care*, about a cavalier who, apart from all sorts of far-fetched adventures in the service of his king, was the owner of a heroic peregrine falcon named Cressida. Well, my bird was not a peregrine but I was a soldier; I was hesitant no longer, her name should be Cressida.

When I looked at her immediately on waking I saw

that not only was she alive but a good deal stronger; she both bit me and struck out with her feet, and seemed even less anxious to make my acquaintance than she had been the previous night. However, she had to be fed, and fed she was despite her protests. This time I gave her a real cropful, and I was getting the knack of feeding her without upsetting her. When I put her back in her basket this time, she shuffled quite happily into a corner, and even started to preen in a lackadaisical way. The fact that she was showing any interest in her appearance was a very hopeful sign. I left her happily at rest, visiting her between parades to see that all was well, and in the evening gave her another enormous meal. I sat on my bed, with Cressida on my knee and Bracken lying beside me on the floor.

For the first time I really looked closely at Cressida who, although only twenty-four hours had passed, seemed to have put on a bit of weight, being firmer and more as a kestrel should be. She was a rich foxy chestnut, barred with black streaks, her breast being flecked with arrow-shaped brown markings. On each side of her face was a dark moustache which gave her a truculent look, like one of Ghengis Khan's nomadic warriors. She didn't look like a young bird, and she was not one of the pair which lived in the Martello tower, for I had seen both of them that afternoon when on firing practice. She seemed happy in her basket, the lining of which I had to change each day. Apart from feeding her I left her alone as much as possible, to avoid spoiling any chance, slight though it might be, of restoring to her the full power of flight. She would sit on my knee after being fed and I could stroke her breast gently with a forefinger. After the first day she never bit or clawed me, and also seemed to know instinctively that Bracken was not interested in birds of prey, whatever she was like with legitimate quarry. John Sheldon had made it clear that he considered the chances of her ever flying were remote, and that any chance would be forfeit if the wing was allowed to move out of position. It was decided that she should remain immobilised for at least three weeks, after which we would know more or less what the future would hold for her.

The days raced by, and though we had not received marching orders we had a pretty shrewd idea of our destination. We guessed that, before we could invade Europe and finally win the war, the Germans would have to be driven out of North Africa, and it seemed probable that we should be called upon to help. Three weeks to the day that Cressida's wing had been set I presented myself at John Sheldon's billet-cum-surgery to get the answer to the question which had been haunting me in every moment that I had had time to think of non-military matters. John was expecting me and, saying little, snipped through the bandage that held Cressida's wings pinioned to her sides.

At that moment John's C.O. came into the sick-bay. He was a medical major who had left a country practice in Lincolnshire at the beginning of the war, and it appeared he always had leanings towards veterinary work. He had heard through the 'bush-telegraph' of the unusual patient due that evening and had come in to offer his advice and help if needed. The wing-tips had been fastened together with strips of adhesive plaster; these were now removed, and the wings well sponged with a damp rag. Cressida was now free. I put her gently on a table and stood back. The injured wing fell forward a trifle and rested on the table-top. None of us said a word. Then she gave a quick hitching movement and the wing went back into place, staying there. She was going to be all right! I picked her up; the doctor gently manipulated the wing, pronounced the fracture mended, and was confident that in time it should be as good as its opposite number.

Cressida showed no concern or relief at the freedom from her bandages, but just sat on the table, peering round her with the curious head-bobbing action that I was to know so well. The muscles of her wings had become slack with the enforced idleness, and there was still considerable bruising, but now at least she could begin to take a more active part in her daily life. That evening, for the first time since we had been brought together, Cressida perched on my fist in the billet surrounded by the members of our platoon, and stuffed herself until her crop stuck out as hard and round as a golf ball. She slept that night perched on the side of the basket a few inches from my head. I woke once and saw her trim streamlined figure in the moonlight, her head resting in the feathers of her shoulder, standing with one foot up and the other clutching the wickerwork. She was deeply asleep, confident that she would not be betrayed, and I felt touched and very happy. Bracken, sensing my wakefulness, stirred quietly and pushed her long muzzle into my hand; she seemed to be saying in her own quiet way: 'I understand how you feel, but please don't forget all about me, we've been together a long time now.' I rubbed her ears, and put my arm round her neck to reassure her. Whatever happened, she would always be number one.

Although Cressida's wing was not broken it was very stiff and she seemed afraid to use it; perhaps it might have been painful. To encourage her I would tilt my left fist on which she was perched so that she had to flap a little in order to keep her balance. I managed to get a pair of old leather gloves from the Q.M. Stores, which made carrying Cressida easier and more comfortable for both of us. All birds seem to prefer to perch on a glove rather than a bare fist. I suppose this could be because leather is vaguely like the bark of a tree, and in any case gives a firmer grip. In the case of hawks the advantage is mutual because all birds of prey, even the smallest, are inclined to grip convulsively when excited, and the result can be uncommonly painful; the more so as the natural reaction is to draw one's hand away, which only induces the bird to grip the harder.

I made a pair of jesses out of a piece of shammy leather and put one on each of her slender yellow legs. This was not to prevent her escape, a feat of which she was then totally incapable, but to stop her crashing to the floor if she overbalanced or attempted to fly to some vantage point in the billet. The jesses were fastened to a three-foot leash, which was attached to the handle of the basket. She was also provided with a block of wood, shaped like an inverted flower-pot, on which she could sit outside during the time I was on duty. We found a sheltered place in what had been the garden of a cottage, and the room orderly made it part of his duty to keep a watchful eye on her. This was especially necessary because envious eyes had already been cast on her by a neighbouring troop of Gunners who wanted her as a mascot.

I noticed that Cressida was becoming increasingly tame, paying little attention when I made my regular inspections, and would sit apparently contentedly as I carried her about on my fist. Her welfare and progress were now a subject of keen interest, and she had a large number of visitors from different companies of the battalion. A few days after the bandages had been taken off I was delighted when she stepped up on to my fist and began feeding straight away.

One day we found some old pieces of corrugated iron lying half buried in the rough tussocky grass; I turned one of these over and found a number of fieldmice. I managed to catch one, killed it, and gave it to Cressida, who delightedly grabbed it in one foot. In about ten minutes it had disappeared, tail and all. Shortly after this I found another, which went the same way as the first. The next morning I found a neat oval pellet in her basket, and Cressida was a different bird. After this, Chollerton and I, together with other members of the platoon, would make regular forays to the pile of old iron which seldom failed to yield up its hidden treasure. I began to carry Cressida everywhere I went off duty and she grew steadily tamer. Then the day came when I put her on top of a five-barred gate and held a piece of meat in my fist three or four inches away and just above her feet. Being very sharp set, after some hesitation she gave a flick with her wings, popped up and began to feed. I tried again, holding my fist nearly a foot away, and once more she flew on to it. Next time I increased the distance to at least three feet; she sidled up and down the gate top, bobbing her head and flexing her wings, then with a sort of flying scramble she cleared the gap, and I let her finish her meal in peace. I knew now that it was only a matter of time before she would be flying again.

I exercised her daily. As soon as duty finished for the day I would call Bracken, and taking Cressida on the fist would hurry off to the land behind the Battalion Area, where we had virtually the whole of Romney Marsh to wander over. As this was, of course, now a restricted area, there were virtually no civilians nearer than Rye which lay a few miles to the west. However, there were rows of rather ugly bungaloid structures which no doubt had been the scene of many a happy family holiday in the peaceful pre-war days. Although the human population was absent there were plenty of other beings to interest us. Hares abounded and were exceptionally stout-hearted and fleet. There were a great many rabbits too. Bracken, who was now five years old, had lost the edge of her speed but she soon reduced the numbers of the rabbits, and she did actually account for a few hares as well, though this was done more by guile than by skill in coursing. Still, that is what she was bred for, and meat of any sort was hard to come by.

We found a pair of owls in a deserted barn, and we once spent many minutes watching a heron, that lone grey sentinel of the marshes, at his fishing. There were ducks galore amongst the weedy reed-fringed dykes, the handsome mallard, the neat and dapper teal, and the shoveller with his great flat bill like an old-fashioned pudding spoon.

Once near a semi-derelict pig-sty Bracken caught a half-grown rat; it must have been nearly as heavy as Cressida, but she demolished it, leaving only the hindquarters and the tail. All this time Cressida's flying powers were increasing; she first came fifty and then a hundred yards to the fist. Her wing was still not quite right and she had a tendency to veer in a half-circle if she had to fly for any considerable distance. Her flight had a curious skimming quality, rather like a boomerang but a good deal more purposeful.

By now Cressida had been more or less accepted by the various echelons of authority within the battalion. My Company Commander showed a friendly interest, and the C.O. would inquire after her health; even the sergeants forbore to let blast with their much-practised strains of military invective, which they reserved for more orthodox occasions. Only the R.S.M. remained unmoved; I think he regarded the presence of a kestrel as unsoldierly, and I suspect he spent hours looking up *King's Regs* to see what they thought about the matter. He must have been disappointed as the keeping of kestrels in the army did not merit a mention. For my part I had to learn how to deal with unexpected contingencies, for example, how to salute an officer whilst carrying a hawk on the fist. Perhaps our ancestors had this in mind when they decreed that hawks should be carried on the left hand. The fact remains that I was not ordered to get rid of the bird; in fact, although this was never admitted, I think Authority took a secret pride in her presence. She soon became used to accompanying me when I rode my bicycle and became adept at balancing, her wings fully extended like a Roman Eagle, as she breasted the breeze caused by our advance.

One weekend leave I pedalled all the way to Heathfield with her. I think the sight of the heavily armed soldier, complete with rifle, tin hat and all the panoply of war, hawk on fist, and a large shaggy dog cantering beside him, must have caused some speculation in the hamlets and villages through which we sped. My mother welcomed the three of us and showed much interest in Cressida. After putting up with me for twenty-two years, I doubt if anything surprised her very much. I had brought rations for Cressida and Bracken as the wartime rations would, of course, not run to even the few ounces of meat they needed each day, but in case of emergencies I seldom travelled without a couple of mousetraps. Cressida slept on the back of a chair in the spare room, surely one of the most unusual guests ever to occupy it. She had by now become so tame that I let her fly up into the branches of the scarlet oak on the lawn and she surprised my mother by flying the length of the garden to my fist at my whistle.

During the afternoon I was carrying her in the wood just across the road when I absentmindedly kicked a rotten stump which I thought might have given refuge to a hibernating slow-worm; as it heaved over there was a flash of reddish fur, and something vanished into the drift of dead leaves. Cressida half flopped, half dived off my fist and crashed all of a heap amongst the leaves. I bent down to pick her up and she started mantling, using her wings like a tent to hide something she was holding in her feet, and at the same time she started scolding me with her high angry kekking scream, the first time she had made a sound since we met. By putting my gloved hand just behind her feet and taking hold of her jesses, I lifted her and her prey on to my fist. She held in her foot a bank vole, her first capture since her accident, and she made it abundantly clear that she meant to keep it all for herself. So I had taken quarry with a kestrel. Not much for the Game Book perhaps, but none the less quarry, and she had taken it fair and square without any hesitation. My mother suggested that I had the mask mounted, a frivolity I might even have complied with if the mask in question had not been in Cressida's crop.

After the capture of the bank vole Cressida's confidence increased, and she soon showed that she was a very courageous bird. She was completely fearless of Bracken, and though at first inclined to bite her nose if the dog tried to sniff her, she soon became more tolerant; later she appeared to show a sort of affinity with the dog, and would sometimes reach down from her perch on a chair and gently tweak her hair as Bracken passed by. Bracken, for her part, had regarded her from the start as part of the family, and the two could be left together for hours on end. There does, in fact, exist a natural affinity between some dogs, especially those of the greyhound breed, and hawks. More particularly falcons seem to reciprocate this feeling. Many years later I was to find that my Arabian Saker falcon, who to the best of my knowledge had never seen a dog before, when introduced to my Saluki showed not the slightest agitation. Within a week or two the pair would work together in a very successful partnership. But this was perhaps hardly surprising as the Arabs have hunted gazelles with a combined team of Salukis and Sakers for centuries.

Cressida would now greet me with her chattering call; when she was sitting in the sun and a feeling of well being overcame her, she would give the well-known kestrel call, generally described as kee-kee-kee. If she suspected that her food was going to be taken away before she had finished it, she would fly into a tantrum, mantle with her wings and shuffle around the floor in a tight circle shrieking abuse, and she would even try to chase me, striking out with the foot that was not grasping the meat. From one so small, this display of temper was so amusing that it never failed to make spectators helpless with laughter. When full fed, or just pleasantly contented with her world, she would 'tick' like the winding-up of a large watch.

She also had a curious habit of burying the uneaten portions of the day's rations and unearthing them later, sometimes much later! During one of my visits to my home I gave her a dead blackbird which I had retrieved from the side of the road. She plucked it and ate it on the paper-covered seat of the large armchair in the spare bedroom which, guests being both rare and unwelcome in wartime, was used as Cressida's occasional 'mews' or roosting place. I cleared up all the mess and feathers she had not swallowed and, having to leave in a hurry, picked up Cressida whose crop was full to bursting and cycled off into the night, in order to be back in camp by lights out. A fortnight or so later, on another visit, I dumped Cressida on the back of her chair and, whilst looking for some paper to cover the seat, saw Cressida jump down on to it. Shuffling about and peering down the cracks she retrieved an extremely unattractive relic of her last forage, which she began to tuck into with relish, showing that she was not over-particular as to the state of her food. I discovered, in fact, that she was as partial to a 'ripe' mouse as a human gourmet is to a well-hung pheasant.

Returning one evening to Camber after exploring the vicinity of Winchelsea, the twin township to Rye, I bought some fish intending to cook it for Bracken. Meat, unless you knew a 'Continental Butcher,' was virtually non-existent, but fish could be obtained at a price even at the most hazardous phase of the war. Although only a private, I was a private with a kestrel; this I soon found gave me a certain mystique, and would occasionally unlock the most unlikely gates, even the gate of the company cook-house. However, it was late and I knew the cook-house would be closed for the night. At this juncture, being on the point of defying the blackout, risking a gipsy-type fire and cooking the stuff myself, I met a soldier, belonging to another unit but bearing beneath his undistinguished battle-dress a heart of purest gold. He knew, as it happened, the one person in Rye who would not only cook, but enjoy cooking, fish for a soldier's lurcher at half-past ten at night. He bade me follow him, which I lost no time in doing.

We climbed up a steep, narrow street and soon reached an old house, covered in ivy, which stood below the jackdaw-haunted ruins of a Norman tower. The owner of the house, Miss Sanderson, was a sort of Universal Aunt to the soldiers who were lucky enough to come within her orbit. She was a tall, dark-haired, happy-go-lucky Irish woman, who made up for the fact that she had no children of her own by mothering anyone whom she felt to be in need. Her house was always full of soldiers, sailors and airmen, for whom she would cook endless meals, manufactured apparently out of nothing. She would wash mountains of grimy, sweaty socks and shirts. She made the best bread I have ever eaten; indeed, there was little that she would not do to cheer and encourage the homesick and the weary-hearted. If ever a civilian deserved a medal for her single-handed efforts to keep up military morale then that civilian was Miss Sanderson.

When I was introduced to her on this first occasion she wasted no time in talking, but took the fish and, whilst it was cooking, arranged a perch for Cressida on a screen in the living-room. She brought cups of tea and introduced me to her protégés who, in the smoky firelit scene, appeared to include half the Southern Command. Refreshed, we went on our way promising to come back the next weekend when Miss Sanderson told us her niece was coming on leave. She made it clear that it was Cressida to whom the invitation really applied. 'After all,' she said, 'soldiers are two a penny, but a hawk as tame as this one you are lucky to see once in a lifetime.' None the less, by off-duty next Saturday I was prepared to travel almost any distance for the chance of a decently cooked meal, if nothing else, and the three of us duly presented ourselves for lunch.

Miss Sanderson's niece turned out to be an uncommonly snappy little W.A.A.F., as Irish as the Halls of Tara, with hair the colour of a copper beech and a brogue that would surely have melted the granite heart of Oliver Cromwell. She soon succumbed to the subtle charm of Cressida and pleased me enormously by mistaking Bracken for an Irish wolfhound, a breed to which, though slightly larger than Bracken, she certainly bore a strong resemblance. She was anxious to see Cressida flying free, being by no means convinced of her much-vaunted obedience. We duly repaired to the nearest convenient part of Romney Marsh for a demonstration. Cressida, being cast off, rose into the wind to a considerable height, the lopsidedness caused by her injury scarcely showing as she circled above our heads. After the performance had been sufficiently admired, I threw out the line which I had recently made and Cressida, awaiting her cue, dropped like a plummet to take her reward, a piece of liver with which the lure was garnished.

Iola, for that was the name of my companion, was, as I had both hoped and expected, highly impressed with the whole thing. On our return, nearing the precincts of the town, I came across a large piece of moribund tarpaulin and turned it over. Amongst the yellow grass and bleached roots that were exposed were not only the usual slugs and centipedes, but a minute and obviously half-fledged field-vole. This I retrieved and handed to Iola, who was enraptured with so attractive a rodent; she carefully wrapped it in her handkerchief and placed it in the breast pocket of her immaculate uniform tunic. Miss Sanderson produced, with the infallibility that was so characteristic of her, a medicine dropper, and soon the infant was sucking up a mixture of diluted condensed milk, cod liver oil and glucose. I gathered that it thrived on this revolting mixture and grew to full voledom; it enjoyed the highly inappropriate but, I suppose, flattering name of Cressida, becoming a popular and honoured member of Iola's W.A.A.F. squadron at Uxbridge.

Chapter 10

During November the battalion moved to Iden Green, near Hawkhurst, a dozen or so miles inland. We marched there in battle array, performing various military manœuvres on the way. Cressida travelled perched on the top of my haversack, with her jesses attached by her leash to the tapes of my gas cape. She soon got used to this mode of transport and would sit happily hour after hour, adjusting her balance to the rhythmic tramp of marching feet and making no attempt to leave her station. But when the company fell out for a short break each hour she would be released, and would then stretch her wings with short flights or even take the opportunity of a quick bath in some convenient roadside puddle, for she always took pride in keeping her plumage in perfect trim. Bracken also revelled in these marches but, if she became tired and footsore, was wise enough to cadge a lift in the transport that accompanied our columns to pick up the halt, the lame, the fainthearted and the just plain idle.

The billets at Iden Green were Nissen Huts, our first experience of this unprepossessing but remarkably comfortable form of accommodation. Cressida preferred this arrangement because she could sleep on the post at the foot of the bunk, which was a two-tiered affair. Luckily the man who slept in the bottom bunk, Private Chollerton, did not mind having a hawk as a near bedfellow, and the three of us arranged things to our satisfaction. Bracken, as was her wont, slept happily curled up on a pile of old sacks in the alleyway between our bunk and the next one. This could have caused some awkward moments at kit inspections, but I generally had time to fasten Bracken to a convenient branch which luckily lay half buried in grass behind the billet and out of sight, while I tucked Cressida inside my battle-dress tunic.

On one occasion there was a visit from the Divisional Commander or some such big-wig. This particular inspection was unexpected; we were all in a bit of a flap, and for the first and, I think, only occasion during our life together I forgot Cressida, who for some reason was sitting on my tin hat at the back of my bed. The C.O., coming round for a preliminary inspection and seeing Cressida, bellowed, 'For God's sake get that bloody bird out of sight or you'll get us all shot!' I grabbed her and perched her on a fence that divided our lines from the woodlands behind. I naturally intended to retrieve her as soon as the inspection was over, but it took longer than usual and when I did go to find her she had gone. This was one of the worst moments of my life; we had only been together for a few weeks, but I had grown extremely fond of her. She also provided an outside interest, and in a curious way seemed to form a link with the more stable world to which I hoped one day to return. I had a quick look for her, but I had to be on parade again in ten minutes. The next parade was unfortunately a route march and I would be away for hours. I asked the billet orderly to do his best to find her and marched away with an empty heart.

I had always enjoyed these route marches. There was an air of informality; men would sing any song that came into their heads, some had mouth-organs with which to enliven the passing hours, we could talk and joke and, of course, it gave one time to think. On this march I thought a lot, and they were not pleasant thoughts. What could have happened to Cressida? How would she cope? I was by no means certain that she could fend for herself. It is one thing for a bird to fly well enough to come from a tree to an artificial lure, but quite another to have sufficient dexterity to catch even such an unsuspicious and comparatively inactive animal as a vole. A kestrel depends a great deal on its ability to hover, an exercise which requires an enormous amount of co-ordination between mind and body, and even the slightest injury to such a vital component as a wing must be an almost insurmountable handicap.

The more I thought about it, the less I liked it. I had no intention whatever of keeping her against her will and if she was fit enough and clever enough to look after herself that would have suited me. But she was, after all, my responsibility; I had plucked her from the marshes and almost certain death, and until I was convinced she no longer needed me I was determined to look after her. My concern may seem somewhat out of proportion considering the enormous issues at stake; yet one of the reasons for fighting was so that we should remain free, free to be individuals, to enjoy our own countryside, and the companionship of our families and friends, human or otherwise.

Immediately the parade was dismissed I ran back to my hut to find out if the billet orderly had any news. He had not, and what little hope I had died within me. The next day was Saturday and I searched and searched, calling and swinging the lure. Several friends came with me and we split up into gangs combing the woods until every inch must have been trodden and re-trodden a dozen times. I was on guard duty that night and as I paraded my beat with rifle and fixed bayonet, I tried not to think too much. On Sunday morning, tired to the point of exhaustion, I went out again; it shows how much Cressida must have meant to all of us, for even those who had been on guard duty with me, and who would have been entitled to a morning in bed, came out with us in one last search. After ten minutes there was a shout, and rushing blindly through the undergrowth I was soon at the place from whence it came.

There stood Corporal Stone pointing upwards; twenty feet or so above our heads, on the bare tip of a stunted oak tree, sat Cressida. She was calling plaintively with her sad little voice, and when I called her and showed her the lure she dropped out of the tree and landed, light as a butterfly, on my fist. She was ravenously hungry and obviously overjoyed to see us again. In fact, she must have been on her way back because we had passed beneath that tree twice on our search the previous afternoon. The rest of the platoon gathered round; they didn't say much, and what they did was somewhat profane, but it was clear that they were nearly as glad as I was to see the prodigal again. I was particularly happy at Cressida's return for two reasons; firstly, and most obviously, because I had missed her a great deal and was worried as to her fate, but even more because Cressida, a wild kestrel at least a year old, had come back to those she knew she could trust and had come to look on as her friends.

That afternoon I called on the Swinburnes with Bracken and Cressida. Cressida was none the worse for her adventures and was, if anything, tamer than ever. Spearman and Millicent had not yet met Cressida, and they were both enthralled with her and the story of how we came to be together. They had a large garden aviary and we thought Cressida might be happy there for an hour or so, sitting in the sun which, considering the lateness of the season, was still pleasantly warm. Cressida, however, had other ideas and soon showed her displeasure by beating against the wire in a frenzy to escape. This was tactless to say the least, but she always had most decided views. To be enclosed in a room with her friends about her was one thing, but to be relegated to an outside prison quite another. So she sat on a pergola in the garden whilst we had our tea inside; she had had enough wandering to last her for some time and was quite content to sit and be admired.

Soon after this the battalion went on ten days' embarkation leave. I took Bracken and Cressida and cycled home for, I thought, possibly the last ten days we might ever spend together. We didn't do much, just walked in the woods, and sat by the fire and talked. We did not talk much about the war, but a great deal of what we should do when it was over, and we were free to lead our own lives again. This was in December 1942 and I did not, of course, know then what the fortunes of war would have in store for me and my companions; but we did know that the Battle of Alamein had been fought and won, that North Africa had been invaded, and it seemed logical that we would be sent to help drive the Germans out of the southern Mediterranean seaboard.

My mother and I used to sit up well into the small hours, whilst Bracken lay at ease in her basket, happy to be with us. My mother was cheerful and did her best to make this, my last leave, a success. She never showed the anxiety she must have felt; her marriage had been a very happy one and my father's early death while on active service must have been much in her mind. As for myself

I was young, I was fit, and I yearned for adventure. More than anything else I wanted to be personally involved, to be in at the end, to know that whatever the outcome I had at least played my part. The thought of being killed in action hardly occurred to me; it was a chance one had to take. What I did dread was the possibility of being blinded; never again being able to see Bracken in full stretch or the flashing stoop of a falcon to the swung lure. Almost as bad was the thought of being a captive, of long years at the mercy of a savage foe, the degradation, and the fear that I might not prove man enough to stand up to interrogation, to the hardships and the hunger. However, although this sort of thing happened to others, surely it could never happen to me?

Whilst on leave I received a message that the battalion had moved once more, this time to Camberley, and that I was to report there after the ten days were up. My mother had offered to look after both Bracken and Cressida, for it was probable that when I returned to the battalion I would get no further chance of contacting her. We had decided to come up to London the night before I was due to report to Cambeley. That evening I said good-bye to Bracken, who knew well enough that something unpleasant was afoot. I cuddled her, bade her guard my home until my return, and gave her a final pat. She came to the door to see me get into the taxi that was to take us to the station, and was still watching as we rounded the corner of the lane. I did not see her again for two and a half years.

Cressida travelled with us in the compartment, sitting on my knee and peering out of the window as the countryside she knew and loved rushed past her. At Victoria the train disgorged us into the crowded hurly-burly of wartime London. I took a firm grip on Cressida's jesses as we hurried through the barrier. Two lance-corporals of the Military Police, the dreaded Red Caps, were lurking there. They looked at me, they looked at Cressida, their mouths opened and shut, but not a word was uttered. I hurried on into the crowds expecting at any moment to feel the heavy hand of authority on my shoulder, but none came. I rejoined my mother and we plunged into the Underground, *en route* for South Kensington.

I had never carried Cressida in public before, except, of course, in Rye, where most people came to know and take an interest in her. Now, whenever we left our house in Montpelier Square, we were seen by crowds of people, many of whom had never seen a live hawk before, and had not the slightest idea as to what manner of bird she might be. We had to put up with some pretty absurd questions such as 'What sort of bird is that, mister, a h'eagle?', 'Can that parrot say anything, mate?', or 'Cor, look at the soldier wiv a carrier-pigeon, taking messages I expect!' This sort of thing was funny at first but became increasingly irritating, until it was an effort to prevent myself replying in a sarcastic and offensive manner.

The next day was to be the last that my mother and I would spend together for some time. I had to catch a train from Waterloo in order to report to the company before midnight, so we decided to dine at one of my mother's clubs. As I would have to leave for the station immediately after the meal we had no alternative but to take all my equipment with me and, of course, Cressida. The club was a very high-class, conservative, even snooty establishment. The doorman took one look at us and hurried off to fetch the secretary. The secretary informed us that he regretted no dogs or birds were allowed on the premises, and I had a feeling that he would have liked to add private soldiers to the list of undesirables. My mother, well able to cope with such contingencies, made a suitably icy retort and tendered her resignation on the spot. The secretary started stammering apologies, but meanwhile we had swept out into the night. We dined instead at the V.A.D. Club, where we were welcomed and where we enjoyed a most excellent meal, during which we talked about every conceivable subject except the war and my immediate future.

As we finished our dinner the air-raid warning sounded and the taxis vanished like melting snow from the streets. At this time London was only subjected to occasional attacks. The Luftwaffe had tried and failed to force the country to its knees the previous winter; such raids were a confounded nuisance, but no longer the ghastly nightmare they had been. We walked the deserted streets until one taxi-driver, bolder than his mates, hove in sight and we eventually arrived at Waterloo to find no trains in sight. I reported to the R.T.O. who stamped my pass, and then the all-clear sounded. My train arrived and, shivering in the bitter cold, I installed myself in a corner seat. Cressida perched on my tin hat in the luggage rack and, no doubt wondering what it was all about, was soon asleep, showing the remarkable adaptability that was so typical of her. The wartime trains were unheated and the going was slow and unpleasant; however, we reached Camberley at some time in the small hours to find the place deserted.

I had no idea where the Sherwood Foresters were billeted, so much against my will I reported to the nearest outpost of Military Police. After inspecting my pass and ascertaining that I was not a deserter or a German spy with a radio concealed in Cressida, they couldn't have been more kind and helpful. They phoned the battalion guard-room to report my arrival, gave me a good meal of bacon and eggs, washed down with gallons of tea, and finally let me sleep until first light on a spare bunk in the guard-room. At dawn we left with mutual good wishes in search of our billets.

These were in a requisitioned private house somewhere on the outskirts of Camberley. Both officers and men were surprised, to say the least, that I had brought Cressida back with me, particularly as the battalion were standing ready to leave at a moment's notice. I suppose, if I had considered the matter at all, I would have admitted that I regarded Cressida not only as a companion but as a sort of talisman, and I felt deep down inside that with her close at hand, each receiving strength and encouragement from the other, things were bound to turn out right in the end. It was a peculiar relationship, but a most satisfactory one.

Apart from roll-calls and hut inspections we had little to do, and were allowed to go more or less our own way, provided of course that we were all present and correct at 11.59 each night. We were now trained to the highest peak of efficiency and I suppose it was considered that we should be allowed to relax, to avoid the danger of staleness setting in. Be that as it may, we were under a minimum of restraint, a state of affairs of which I believe no one took advantage. I used to take Cressida for exercise in the grounds of the R.M.C. at Sandhurst, bordering the main London Road. Here I would cast Cressida to the winds and watch elated as she rose on fleeting wings, and wait till she was a tiny black cross in the sky, seeming no bigger than a swallow. She would circle and glide leaning on the wind, then sweep in a great arc high above my head. Her high chattering call, softened by wind and space, would come down to me as she revelled in the freedom of her own element until, her energy spent, she would drop almost with the speed of a peregrine to take the lure or, after making a circle of the park, would skim in to land on my fist with as little impact as a bunch of wind-blown thistledown.

One afternoon I had called her down after one of her most spectacular aerial displays, during which I had become completely lost to the world. She had just come back to the fist and was being fed, when I became aware that I was not alone. Turning round I saw a splendid figure, ablaze with glittering brass and bright with scarlet tabs. I drew myself rigidly to attention, while Cressida was still feeding herself on my left fist, and snapped out the salute of a lifetime. The general, as this resplendent being proved to be, quickly put me at my ease. He told me how much he had enjoyed the performance, asked me a few questions about Cressida's history, and with a friendly smile strode through the gates and was gone, leaving me a shaken but a proud and happy man.

There was a tenseness in the air and we were living on our nerves; we knew what we were about to be called upon to do, and we wanted to get on with it with as little delay as possible. Our feelings must have been rather like those of riders in the Grand National as they line up for the start, a mixture of excitement, impatience and even fear, as well as a natural desire to show their mettle and what they were capable of achieving.

I was having dinner with a friend when news came that orders had come at last, and we were on our way. Back in the billets all was confusion as we hurried about collecting our equipment and mustered in the street for our final roll-call. Officers and N.C.O.s bustled about with their torches, dimly directed downwards to the papers they held in their hands. We fell in in three ranks and after we had been counted and recounted, the command to march came at last, and we turned and swung off to the right, our column moving through the blacked-out streets of Camberley. There was hardly a sound to indicate the passing of many hundreds of men; the muffled tread, the orders quietly given, just the clink of a rifle butt touching the brass fittings of webbing equipment. So the 2/5 Sherwood Foresters marched out to war.

The train lay dark and silent, looking like a great dormant serpent in its siding as we climbed in and piled our rifles and steel helmets in the racks. Cressida was sitting, one leg hidden in her breast, on my tin hat, and I looked at her as she preened happily, pulling the tips of her primary feathers through her beak; bringing her tail round so that she could get at it properly, she gave it a thorough grooming, then began to smooth the feathers of her breast. Her toilet completed to her satisfaction, she shook herself like a dog. As she did so one tiny breast feather came fluttering down like a snowflake. I caught it before it landed and put it carefully in my breast pocket.

Well, the die was cast for good or ill; Cressida was coming with us.

Chapter 11

THE train snorted, lurched, and slowly started to move, and gaining speed was soon racing between the silent moonlit fields of Surrey. Once the train started moving northwards we settled in our seats. Cigarettes were handed round, packs of cards were produced, and soon my companions were, or so it seemed, as happy and relaxed as if the train was carrying them on leave instead of rushing them towards an unknown and certainly unpleasant destination, from which it was probable many would never return. I looked about me at my comrades; they were good-hearted, humorous, level-headed and courageous, each man with his own special philosophy, and I felt a surge of warmth and genuine affection. They were my mates, and whatever happened, whatever the discomforts and the dangers that lay ahead we were all in it together. And there, perched above us asleep on her chosen point of vantage, was Cressida, the Sussex kestrel, who had thrown in her lot with us. As I watched her swaying gently with the motion of the train I made a vow that, come what might, I would take care of her and, God willing, bring her safely home again.

The talk died down as each man, seeking what comfort he could, relaxed and, leaving worries to the morrow, slept as only soldiers can. I managed to sleep for some hours, to wake stiff and freezing in the icy winter dawn. There were shouts and the sound of trolleys being pushed up and down the platforms. All about me were men stretching and yawning, as they fought their way back into full consciousness. Someone pulled aside the black-out curtain at the carriage window. On the platform stood a trolley full of cups of steaming tea, under the minis-trations of a smiling green-uniformed member of the W.V.S. Never has tea been more welcome or tasted sweeter. It stirred sluggish blood and made even Liver-pool at 7 a.m. on a December morning seem just about tolerable.

This, it appeared, was the end of our train journey; already groups of men were lining up on the platform. Somehow I struggled into my equipment, grabbed my rifle, picked up a sleepy and rather indignant Cressida, and hurried out into the murk and drizzle. N.C.O.s were patrolling the platform like sheep-dogs rounding up their reluctant charges. Eventually our company was collected into some sort of order, and the inevitable roll called; it seemed no one had deserted. An army truck appeared, and breakfast was served. I sat on my kit-bag and some-how forced down mouthfuls of cold bacon and bread, followed by more cups of tea. I unwrapped a piece of meat and gave it to Cressida who was now showing some interest in her surroundings. She ate a hearty breakfast; nothing it seemed could impair her appetite. I had taken the precaution of acquiring enough fresh raw meat to last several days. This had been given to me by a friendly butcher in Camberley for just such an eventuality. It was wrapped up in a piece of parachute silk, which I hoped would help to preserve its freshness until I could come by something better.

After breakfast we formed up once more, and struggling with kit-bags and all the rest of our impedimenta we shuffled to the quayside where, riding the oily water, looming big, black and forbidding in the half light was our transport, the good ship *Derbyshire*. As I stared morosely at this hideous hulk I thought wistfully of happy journeys of the past; of the *Aquitania*, and how as a schoolboy of eight or nine I had been welcomed on the bridge and had even been allowed to hold the wheel of that luxurious leviathan. I thought of the sturdy little cross-channel ferries that had shepherded us across from Southampton to Cherbourg on our annual trips to the Continent. It was abundantly clear that this was not to be a luxury voyage.

A group of Liverpudlian dockers appeared and were soon exchanging witticisms with my companions. I would have liked to be friendly with them too, but I could not understand a word they said. This was unfortunate as I yearned for some last contact with my native land. However, I didn't need an interpreter to see that they thought Cressida a fine bird, and were amazed that she was coming with me. More orders were given and now platoon after platoon marched up the gangplank, longing to put on some sort of show which, if the others felt as I did, took a bit of doing. I paused at the top of the gangway and looked back with Cressida nestling against my cheek. I took a deep breath and followed the others deep into the bowels of the ship. It was Christmas Eve, 1942.

Our accommodation, if it could be called that, was on E Deck which was, or seemed to be, as far below as it was possible to go without finding oneself up to the neck in bilge water. We slept in hammocks, which may be all right for sailors, but the heat, the lack of air, the glaring artificial light and above all the noise of the ship's engines and the motion of the ship did not make me yearn for a life on the ocean wave. Cressida settled quite happily on the rope from which the hammock was suspended, and within half an hour or so distinguished herself by slaying a young rat that was unwise enough to show itself from behind a pile of paper. Judging by its condition it had fared very well, and Cressida's rations were attended to at least for that day. Though feeling depressed and homesick I noticed, nevertheless, that the rat was not a common rat but the rarer black or ship's rat, the cause of the Black Death, a smaller species that had been reduced by its larger and more ferocious kinsman to the point of extermination, but which still managed to maintain a foothold in docks, warehouses and the holds of ships. This specimen was certainly in its right setting.

After all the men and baggage had embarked we were free to explore the ship. I climbed up endless companionways until at last I reached fresh air, and stood leaning against the rails watching the rows of herring-gulls sitting on the roofs of the various wharfs and customs sheds. I envied them; they didn't have to sleep in a smelly, stuffy and overcrowded hold. It occurred to me at this point that Cressida too might have had a change of heart. If she wanted to leave me this was perhaps the last chance she would have. On a sudden impulse I cut through her jesses with the penknife I always carried. I put her on the ship's rail facing the land and walked away without looking back; I couldn't bear to see her leave. I heard her calling, but kept on walking. I had to climb over some obstruction on the deck and glanced back. Cressida had already come half the distance between us; I held up my gloved fist and she glided on to it, at once lifting one of her feet and tucking it into her breast feathers, a sure sign of contentment. My conscience was clear, and together we went below.

All that day we lay at anchor, but at dusk there were signs of activity. The crew of the *Derbyshire* seemed to consist mostly of Lascars and other less identifiable orientals with a handful of ordinary British seamen. Now there was bustle and confusion; the engines began to chug, the ship to vibrate, ropes were cast off and so slowly as to be hardly noticeable the bows swung out into the glutinous, soupy green waters of the Mersey. I was standing with most of the platoon lining the rails. None of us spoke. A crowd had gathered at the dockside to see us off, and through the gloom a few white handkerchiefs fluttered; shouts wishing us God speed and Happy Christmas reached us over the widening gulf. Then suddenly someone began to sing 'We'll Meet Again,' others took it up, and soon the whole troopship and quayside echoed with it. The blanket of evening came down as the *Derbyshire* drew out towards the Irish Sea, and still those voices, softened by distance, came to speed us on our way.

Of that voyage the less said the better. Within twenty-four hours of leaving Liverpool Old Father Neptune began to show his hand and the *Derbyshire*, not to be outdone, did everything except turn herself inside out. I took to my hammock and remained there in a semi-coma, unable to eat, drink or even sleep, and I was only vaguely aware of my surroundings. I know that once a day we were summoned for life-boat drill, but I was physically incapable of attending this and so, I discovered later, were many of my companions. Nevertheless, once every twenty-four hours I used somehow to collect enough strength to stagger to the galley where the ship's cook, a most worthy fellow, took pity on my plight and gave me liver and other delicacies, no doubt intended for the captain's table. I was just able to lurch and struggle back again where the sight of Cressida, stuffing herself with unabated eagerness, was enough to bring on fresh paroxysms of a suffering so intense that at times I longed for a torpedo to send us to the bottom, where at least the interminable motion would cease and I would be at peace.

The trip could have lasted days, weeks or months for all I knew. At last I became dimly aware that things had improved slightly, the ship was no longer bucking and plunging like a harpooned whale, but was gliding serenely on her way. After a few hours, during which I feared that I was imagining the relief, and that the ship would soon hurl herself into even greater contortions, I dragged myself from my hammock. With others equally afflicted, I crawled up the companion-ways until the sea wind caught us full in our faces and restored us in a few minutes to some semblance of human beings.

We were in the Mediterranean, Gibraltar was behind us and Africa close on our starboard bow; around us for the first time we saw the other ships of our convoy, and a brave sight they made. In and out, dolphin-like, flashed the twin destroyers, whooping like gibbons as they guarded our flanks, keeping their weather eyes always alert for signs of U-boats. It was sunny, the sea sparkled, and somehow life had lost some of its grimness. I sat in a sheltered corner of the deck, watching the sea and peering out to where just over the horizon lay the coast of Africa.

I had brought one book with me, *The Flax of Dreams*, by Henry Williamson. It took up practically all the spare space in my haversack, but it proved a most adaptable and inspiring companion. I propped myself up in a corner and was soon lost in the boyhood adventures of young Willie Maddison as the *Derbyshire* steamed resolutely eastwards. We knew officially by now that we were heading for Algiers, the former stronghold of Vichy France, which had been cleared of enemy occupation by a landing made earlier in the autumn. Soon the ship drew towards the shore and there lay Algiers itself, terrace upon terrace of white-painted French colonial houses, intermingled with Arabian mosques and minarets. I thought once more of *Beau Geste* and was thankful that our N.C.O.s did not include the evil and sadistic Colour-Sergeant Lezanne.

Soon the ship lay alongside, the gangway was lowered, and still somewhat shaky we formed up on deck. I fell in with the rest, Cressida on my fist and excitement in my heart. We trooped down the gangway and formed up in platoons on the quayside; we were on African soil at last. Africa, the land I had always longed to visit, the land I had thought about, read about and dreamed about, and here I was in person. I looked at Cressida, lazily stretching herself and revelling in the late afternoon sun; our real adventures were about to begin. All around us other ships were disgorging their human cargoes. There were British, Americans, Free French, Canadians; just about every conceivable allied nation was represented, as were most branches of the armed forces.

Finally the order came to march. Out through the suburbs of Algiers we went, along the white dusty roads under the scattered palm trees; the bright sunny afternoon gave place to dusk, dusk to star-encrusted night. The European winter lay far away; it could have been another world. On we went between the orange groves, past the gnarled and twisted shapes of ancient olive trees. The gloom, the sickness and the discomfort were forgotten. We were infantry, the P.B.I., and if there was one thing we could do it was to march. A few kilometres out of Algiers the small Franco-Arab town of Maison-Carrée nestled amongst dusky cypress trees and great clumps of date palms. We marched through the square, where the silence was broken only by the fluting calls of Scops owls in the huge plane trees; on and on again we trudged, halting at last at a deserted brickworks about which were a few Arab hovels, forming the settlement of Barraque.

Here were to be our temporary quarters; here we would wait and hold ourselves in readiness to move into the front line in the hills of distant Tunisia. The brickworks was a curious place, like a gigantic honeycomb with walls of bricks and tiles rising from ground level until they were lost to sight in the shadowy darkness of the roof. The walls of bricks were arranged like old-fashioned manorial dove-cotes with small rectangular spaces all the way up. These niches made ideal receptacles for equipment, packets of cigarettes and other small possessions. One such cubby hole soon became a nightly resting-place for Cressida, who was as much at home here as she would have been in any natural cavity in a cliff or quarry.

While at Barraque the battalion did very little in the way of parades. We turned out each morning for roll-call and rifle inspections and had the odd equipment check; other than this we were more or less free to lie in the sun and barter our almost unsmokable Victory V cigarettes for eggs and tangerines. In the afternoons I would take Cressida on long exploratory walks. I would cast her off and let her take as much exercise as she wished, after which I would call her down from the sky. The country being flat and open suited her style of flight to perfection. She could rise and make great ranging circles until almost lost from sight, and there high in her element would fairly burn up the sky. She seemed as light and speedy on the wing as any peregrine, and would stay aloft just for the pure joy of flight and to feel the gentle Mediterranean breezes blowing through her primaries. She would 'wait on' above my head and when the expected lure was thrown would swing down in easy stages, never in a hurry, until at tree-top level or thereabouts she would plunge into the grass for her well-merited award.

The grass was full of grasshoppers, crickets and small mentids. One of the grasshoppers was the exact replica of a piece of sun-dried hay, yellow, frail and wispy; another, a most impressive beast, was a huge green insect bigger than the locust, the females carrying a great curved ovipositor like a miniature rhinoceros horn. There were glossy black scarab-type beetles, which appeared condemned to the Herculean task of struggling through their own grass jungle with huge balls of dried dung. Cressida was in a kestrel gourmet's paradise. She would continually flop off my fist into the grass to grab a fat and succulent grasshopper; holding it in one foot she would then methodically remove the wing cases and hind legs, which she would discard in a most casual manner. I once watched her devour eighteen of the grasshoppers in the course of a short afternoon walk.

These free-flying interludes were not without their moments of hazard. One afternoon, when Cressida was well on the wing and at least four hundred yards away, I heard a low scolding kek, kek, kek, and turned to see a large falcon, a lanner I think, stooping at her with the speed of light. I shouted and threw my forage cap in the air; Cressida saw the falcon and dived for the cover of a group of cork-oak trees. The falcon pressed home the stoop and Cressida sideslipped in the nick of time. The falcon threw up, turned over and stooped again; Cressida, out of training for such a contest, jinked like a hare, hurled herself on to her back in a furrow and with her feet prepared to defend her life dearly. The falcon saw me and hearing my shouts swung round, climbed in a great arc and made for a line of distant hills from which she had no doubt started on her hunting foray. Cressida, panting like a grampus, jumped on to my fist and I carried her to a convenient stream so that she could drink and regain her shattered composure.

Birds of prey were common here; I saw a small scattered flock of black kites drifting aimlessly overhead one afternoon, and on another occasion when I was sitting in the sun just outside the brickyard Cressida, who was perched on a pile of rubble enjoying a dust bath, began to chatter excitedly. I looked up just in time to see a magnificent red kite sail past so close that I could admire the lavender-grey head and rapacious eye, the colour of old ivory. The breeze was stirring the great widely forked tail, which seemed almost to play the part of an extra wing. At dusk one evening, returning from a walk with Private

Chollerton, a huge owl rose a few yards ahead of us and floated off into the gloom. This excited me more than anything and I wondered if it could have been an eagle owl and if the species occurred so far south. This unsolved mystery has intrigued me ever since.

Algeria had a much more sinister side. The town of Maison-Carrée had an atmosphere of evil, that was more easily experienced than described. One felt that all sorts of dark deeds were going on behind the tall windowless houses that lined the streets, whose roofs almost met overhead. In daylight this was bad enough, but at night even the shadows seemed to come alive. One night a group of us were returning to the brickyard after an evening at the local *estaminet* where we had met and enjoyed the company of a party of French commandos. As we passed through a narrow alleyway on the outskirts of the town we heard shuffling footsteps behind us, and glancing round we saw dark furtive figures detach themselves from the shadows and follow too closely for comfort. We turned together and cocked our rifles; the figures fell back, but as we continued on our way we heard them take up the pursuit again. It was almost pitch dark and the air was heavy with the peculiar foetid smell so common in North African towns. On hearing whispering ahead of us we fixed bayonets, and with two of us facing about in case of attack from the rear, we slowly worked our way down the street. At last we were clear of the town and paused to light cigarettes; we were all sweating with the strain of the experience. Later we heard that a number of Americans returning alone at night had disappeared without trace. This was not an enjoyable end to a pleasant evening.

When the orders came at last to move up to the front I found it almost an anticlimax. Everything was very quiet and orderly; all signs of excitement had died down and this was just another day to get through somehow. We marched to the station at Maison-Carrée and entrained in cattle wagons of the type used in the 1914–18 war. We climbed in, dumped our equipment and made ourselves as comfortable as possible; there was at least a covering of straw on the floor. I leaned my rifle in a corner, balanced my tin hat on top of the muzzle, and put Cressida on top of the lot. I wished I had had the chance to photograph her in this position. Luckily I had the time and forethought to collect a tin of large locust-like grasshoppers for her, so she would not go hungry. This put my mind at rest, because none of us knew how long the journey was going to take or what would await us at the end of it. It was hot and sultry in the wagons with the noonday sun beating down with full force, doing its best to fry us alive. Fortunately most of us had a pack-ful of oranges and tangerines, and those who had not shared in the loot.

After the usual delays and frustrations the train at last got under way with groans and jolts, one so shattering that it brought my rifle, tin hat and Cressida down on top of me. The railway, a single-track affair, wound its way through the richly cultivated coastal belt, past forests of stunted cork trees, and finally began to climb into the hills, which appeared to be covered with some kind of heath or heather.

We passed through some splendid country and I thought to myself how much I would enjoy returning here one day and exploring it at my leisure. We travelled on eastwards throughout the night and the following day, pulling up sometimes at wayside halts where we bought dates, fruit and eggs from the swarthy and unattractive quasi-Arabs that were always hanging around these places. At last, after fully twenty-eight hours in these cramped and uncomfortable wagons, the train came to a halt; we had reached the railhead.

Out we climbed and once more arranged ourselves with the usual paraphernalia until we looked like over-loaded Christmas trees. We formed up and prepared to march, but just in time the company transport lorries arrived. Mugs of tea were served, and how we enjoyed it! I looked towards the great slopes of Greenhill and Baldie. How well we were to know those hills before much time had passed. As I watched, the sky was suddenly illuminated by a bright eerie light which hung poised like a dying star before fading into nothing and leaving the night seeming blacker than before. Only a few miles distant were the enemy. It was a strange and sobering thought that out there in the darkness were thousands of men, wakeful and silent, dedicated to one object, to kill. They would kill me without the slightest compunction, without a second thought, and yet I might have much in common with many of them. However, I was not here to think; our aims were the same. Meanwhile the lorries had unloaded a great pile of wooden crates containing rations, which were to be our main source of nourishment from now on.

I slipped Cressida inside my battle-dress tunic, a procedure which she had come to accept without protest. Here she was warm, safe and quiet, and she would lie down with her feet thrust out in front of her and sleep like a puppy, quite unaware of what might be going on around her. It was time to move off into the front line. Each man seized the handle on one side of a ration box while his mate took the other. With rifles slung over our shoulders, packs on our backs, we heaved and floundered like water buffaloes, cursing softly as we stumbled and lurched up the rocky trail that took us to the cactus-strewn hills of Tunisia where our dug-outs awaited us. These had been occupied by Free French Commandos and were, in fact, great rabbit warrens dug out of the hillside, with all sorts of alcoves where equipment could be stored. They were remarkably well concealed, so much so that it was easy to miss them altogether and blunder off into enemy territory.

These dug-outs were reasonably comfortable, very much more so than those experienced by an earlier generation in Flanders. There was, however, one feature common to both, which soon made itself unmistakably and unpleasantly obvious. They were lousy. It is difficult to describe to those who have not experienced it just how loathsome and degrading it is to share one's clothes, day and night, with a host of parasites. Apart from the irritation there is the inescapable feeling of self-contempt. We used to spend hours sitting in the sun picking the disgusting creatures out of the seams of our shirts; we did our best to keep them down, but it was a never-ending battle. At the Rest Camp, a few miles down, was a de-infestation unit and here, with the aid of D.D.T., we managed to keep this demoralising and ever-present enemy within some sort of bounds.

The dug-outs themselves occupied the slope of one of the many low hills which characterised this part of North Africa; a few miles to the north-east lay Greenhill and Baldie, which at this time were in the hands of the enemy. The Leicesters, Lincolns, Yorks and Lancs were similarly situated on our left and right flanks, and behind us in support were the Royal Artillery. These Gunners would amuse themselves by frequent duels with the Germans; thus our lines were made interesting by the whistle and whine of shells passing over our heads in one direction or another. Of course there was no guarantee that one of these missiles would not fall short and disturb the comparatively even tenor of our lives. Cressida from the first was quite disdainful of artillery fire and not unduly worried about rifles or bren guns either.

Near my dug-out there was a great moss-covered boulder, and the hollow behind it was the home of a family of small lizards, a form of skink, each distinctively marked with a horizontal white stripe running the length of its body. They used to come out at almost exactly the same time each morning to sun-bathe. Cressida was determined to reduce their numbers, and would sit with her feathers wrapped tightly around her, her head bobbing with anticipation and excitement, until she estimated that one of the lizards was far enough from cover; then she would drop on it without a sound. However the lizard, must have had some sort of warning system, for as far as I know she never caught one.

There was a tiny crystal-clear mountain stream flowing down the side of our particular piece of Tunisia, and Cressida used to spend a lot of time drinking, bathing and paddling in one of the shallow pools that were formed in the hollows on the way down the hillside. She had another habit that I have never seen in any of my other birds of prey; after shuffling about in the wet sandy gravel beside one of these pools she would pick up and swallow one or two small pebbles. These were later regurgitated in the same way as she produced her castings and were similarly coated with slime. They must have aided her digestion, but I admit that I was rather worried the first time I saw her doing this. Although as usual she enjoyed complete freedom, she seldom strayed far from the area of my dug-out. Apart from the boulder home of the skinks her favourite look-out was an enormous prickly pear cactus, which was the last place I would have expected her to choose.

Chapter 12

ONE night I was selected to go on night-patrol, to find out if certain territory was occupied by the enemy. This was my first experience of genuine action, and I was duly excited and nervous as zero hour approached. We blackened our faces commando-fashion, wore rubber-soled boots for stealth, and carried sten guns, a weapon which personally I never liked or trusted. They seemed to have the habit of either firing at the slightest jolt or else jamming without apparent reason and refusing to fire at all. However, I hoped mine was in a reasonable frame of mind that night. I had the enviable position of 'Lucky Charlie,' the chap who, following some way behind the main body of the patrol, had to report back to H.Q. if the others were shot or captured.

At zero hour we stole out from our area, single file, heading towards the heights to the north-east, where we supposed the enemy were operating. Although we had rehearsed many times for such a patrol it was an exciting business. We moved, half-crouching, avoiding the sky-line; halting, listening, then gliding on once more. Every cactus grove could conceal an enemy—every isolated bush seemed to resemble the outline of a German helmet. However, as we moved forward and nothing happened we grew more confident, a confidence greatly increased in my case by the feel of Cressida's warm feathery body pressed close against me, as she lay dozing inside my battle-dress tunic. I had taken her at the last moment, for it occurred to me that if I were wounded, or had to escape on my own, I might have to hide in the hills for some days before being able to return to H.Q., and there would have been no one to look after her and give her the attention she deserved. However, this time we neither saw nor heard the enemy and returned safely to our lines. I did a number of these patrols; in fact, it was our main nightly activity. Once our patrol did run into the enemy, but our numbers were superior and, being just that bit quicker on the draw, we smote them hard and got away unscathed. This was my first taste of blood, and it gave me the most peculiar feeling. I had shot and probably killed members of my own species; furthermore, I had escaped being killed myself. This was fate, the way things were meant to be, and besides this was the whole reason for my being there. It was easy to become philosophical about the whole business.

After some time in the front line we were sent back to the rest camp to de-infest and rid our clothes of vermin.

Here we had comparatively well-cooked food, steaming hot from the field kitchens; we could buy fruit, and above all we could sleep in comfort knowing it was unlikely that we should be disturbed in the small hours by an unwelcome visit from ill-mannered herrenvolk.

One day I was walking in the cork-oak woods that surrounded the rest camp and saw an enormous tortoise, quite the largest I have ever seen; its shell was a patchwork of orange and olive-green, unlike the pathetic specimens we see in the average British pet shop. Suddenly I heard a shout and turning saw the familiar figure of my old friend, John Sheldon, who had set Cressida's wing for me and set her on the road to recovery and her present adventures. It appeared that John had travelled in the same convoy as us and was now based at the rest camp, where he had the unromantic job of helping to delouse thousands of verminous soldiery. He was amazed to see that Cressida was still with me, although he had heard that we had sailed from Liverpool. We spent a pleasant hour or two together, and agreed that if we both survived we would meet for a celebration dinner as soon as the war was over. We never saw each other again.

Back in the dug-outs life went on as before; we carried out routine patrols, but apart from occasional shells passing overhead there was little evidence of our proximity to the enemy. However, one night I was lying outside my dug-out on a sort of rampart which was used in daylight to form a bren gun post; our patrol had not returned, and I lay for some time watching the silhouetted figure of the sentry, Private Pinnock, who happened to be on guard at that time. I rose and joined him and we had a long chat; we talked about our homes and what we would do if and when we ever returned. I then tried to sleep but lay wakeful, listening to the musical calls of the Scops owls in the valley below, like the striking of tiny hammers on a silver anvil. These made me even more restless; I had never seen a Scops owl, the second smallest owl in

the European list, and now there was a chance to watch them at their hunting.

I put on my rubber-soled shoes, took my rifle, and set off down the hillside. It was a perfect night, the sort of night one dreams of but so seldom experiences. The moon was riding high in the sky, playing hide-and-seek with the scurrying clouds; there was just enough breeze to stir the tips of the olive trees and to stir me to full wakefulness. I reached a belt of trees about half a mile from our position and climbed into the fork of a huge cypress, concealing myself as best I could in the gap where the trunk divided. Here I crouched motionless. A dark, long-winged shape, noiseless as the night, glided out of the shadows and perched a few feet above my head. It was a Scops owl. It dropped to the ground to seize some insect in an open space where the track divided, one path mounting towards our positions and the other bearing left and leading to the higher hills in the distance. I sat silently for some minutes listening to the sounds of the night; the crickets and cicadas, with their intermingled shrilling and buzzing; the tinkling of the tiny stream and once the far distant, quickly repeated, yapping bark of a hunting jackal. This was Africa, unchanged for thousands of years and utterly indifferent to the fortunes and quarrels of mankind.

As I listened I heard the faintest sound of shuffling footsteps. I switched the safety catch of my rifle to the firing position and waited. Round the corner of the path, just visible in the dappled moonlight, came in single file a line of silent figures. Our patrol returning to the lines? I sat motionless, my rifle covering the file, until they were almost directly below the tree where I was perched. I was just on the point of jumping from the tree and hailing them as comrades, when I heard a sudden half-whispered command. It was in German. The patrol never even glanced at the group of trees just above them where I crouched; in seconds they had passed me. I slowly raised my rifle again and made a split-second decision; if the patrol took the right fork leading to our position I would fire. I reckoned I could cause enough confusion and casualties to put them off their probable attempt to make a raid on our lines. If they took the left fork they would be returning to their own lines and could do no further harm that night. I knew that the time I had reached the tree was 0130 hours, the time any self-respecting patrol should have completed its nightly foray and be on its way back to base.

The Germans reached the fork, and my finger was about to take the first pressure. I could hardly resist the urge to fire, but as fate would have it they took the left fork and were soon out of sight amongst the scrubby cactus groves. I lowered my rifle and I cannot to this day be certain if I was more disappointed or relieved at the outcome. I dropped out of the tree and sped back to the lines, where I was challenged by the sentry, who did not appear particularly surprised at my sudden appearance out of the night. I reported on what I had seen and done.

The O.C. could hardly make up his mind whether to congratulate me on my presence of mind and the information I had gathered, or to have me court-martialled for being absent without leave.

We, in our dug-outs in the hills, heard all sorts of rumours and counter-rumours; the enemy were either in full retreat from the Eighth Army who were about to take Tunis, or else were about to counter-attack us, the First Army, in an all-out attempt to drive us back to Algiers. I, like the others in our company, did what I was told, but thought a good deal. One day we heard that the enemy were advancing in overwhelming numbers. We marched to the road below the hillside in which our dug-outs were situated, climbed into immense troop-carrying transport, and drove westward all night and most of the following day. It was an excruciatingly uncomfortable journey, and the only one of us who appeared thoroughly contented was Cressida, who slept as soundly as if she had been perched on a branch of the scarlet oak in our Sussex garden. Towards dusk of the second day we halted for no apparent reason, turned about and returned, eventually reaching our dug-outs again to find them exactly as we had left them, lice, bed-bugs and all.

A day or so later I was sitting on the edge of a weapon-pit drinking a mug of tea and watching a pair of Sardinian warblers, delightful birds like brightly coloured British blackcaps but altogether smarter, their bright carmine eyes giving them an almost ludicrous air of ferocity. They were very confiding and would pick up biscuit crumbs from within a yard of one's feet. Cressida used to sit on her boulder, her head on one side, watching them with an almost benign expression and certainly never made any attempt to chase them. These, the Scops owls, and a pair of large reddish brown buzzards, which could have been long-legged buzzards or perhaps a local subspecies of the ordinary European buzzard, were almost the only birds we saw in these hills.

I had just finished my tea, and was about to visit the cook dug-out for another, when a sudden burst of machine-gun fire came from away on our right flank; this was followed by another and another, until the hills were crackling with the sharp angry rattle. We grabbed rifles, dived into weapon-pits, loaded and prepared the bren gun for action, picked up a number of hand-grenades apiece and stood ready. The shooting, so sudden and unexpected, slowly died down and finally stopped. It was so long since anything drastic had happened that we had begun to wonder, even to hope, that perhaps nothing would happen and that the Germans would, like the Arabs, just quietly fold up their tents and silently steal away. It had been like the phony war all over again on a smaller and more personal scale. Now we all knew, though few would admit it, that this was the real thing at last.

We were in a pretty hopeless position; the enemy held all the high ground above us and could fire on us with ease from these vantage points, and that was exactly what they did. Though of course we did not know this, the Hermann Goering parachute division, one of the toughest and most seasoned bodies of troops in the German Army, had been dropped during the night and we were virtually surrounded. The 40th Division, our division, were all good soldiers, but few of us had seen action before and we had been caught with our trousers down. We spread ourselves out and brought up our bren gun. Then we waited for the enemy to show up, but there wasn't a sign of them although now it was obvious that we were their target. Bits of metal started to fly overhead, some of it too close to be amusing; the frustrating thing was that we could not retaliate, because there was nothing to see. We fired a burst from the bren gun from time to time and let off a few rounds from our short Lee Enfields and Ross rifles in the general direction where we thought the opposition would be. We wanted a chance to get to grips with the enemy, but realised that ammunition was not unlimited and so restrained our urge to fire.

I was fully occupied with the business afoot, looking out for signs of the enemy, and had little time to think of much else. Then I remembered Cressida. Where was she, and what had happened to her? Hardly daring to look, I glanced at her boulder. There she sat, steady and unruffled as a piece of reddish brown granite. The din was by now ear-splitting and the firing unceasing. But Cressida was as imperturbable as the Tower of London. Her steadfast courage amazed me. Here was a wild bird, a member of the shyest and most nervous bird families, who moreover only a few months before had been rescued from a slow death from injury, starvation and exposure. Well, one thing was quite clear; her career would be brought to a speedy end if she remained where she was.

As I watched, a burst of machine-gun bullets skimmed by her side to rip open a large cactus just above and behind her. She lowered her head slightly, as little concerned as if she had been mobbed by our local mistle thrushes at home. Expecting to see her disintegrate at the next burst of firing, I hurriedly produced a chicken leg, left over from a fowl I bought from an Arab a day or two before, which I had intended feeding her on as soon as I had finished that cup of tea. She took a look at it with her usual air of lofty condescension and glided over to our weapon-pit to accept the offering. Battle or no battle she must have her rations. I wished I had a camera to record this unique picture. When her crop was full I grabbed her unceremoniously and perched her on a branch in what I hoped was the most sheltered part of the weapon-pit. Here she sat preening and stretching herself lethargically after her meal.

The firing was heavier than ever now – and then we saw them! The whole of the hill above us was alive with running figures, darting from cover to cover; making use of every cactus bush and the smallest furrow in the open.

They threw everything they had at us, but now at least we had a target and could retaliate and relieve some of our pent-up rage and excitement. There was a continuous fusillade of rapid fire from our rifles; the bren gunners expended magazine after magazine, until the barrels of their weapons were near molten with the heat; the mortar men, thoughtless of range and elevation, plastered everything they could see; and the anti-tank gunners put their anti-tank rifles to an unusual though none the less efficient use.

The enemy must have been under the impression that we had all been wiped out before they started their attack, and must have regretted their impetuosity. The first advance died out and as far as one could see those taking part just ceased to exist. They vanished into the scrub like grouse before the peregrine's stoop. Looking round I took stock of our position. It wasn't pretty; our casualties were heavy, and they were my friends and comrades in arms, men with whom I had trained and shared all the affinities of the strange, close companionship of army life in wartime. I did not have long to reminisce. The firing broke out again, and this time it was even heavier as a fresh wave of German troops reached the crest of the hill above us. We were sitting-ducks, and although we fired hard with all we could muster, we were out-numbered, out-gunned and out-flanked. We had to fall back down the hill. I made time to take Cressida from the weapon-pit and tuck her into my tunic and then, with only my rifle and as much ammunition as I could grab, I joined the others. I found a convenient piece of rock rising from the scrub, and ducked behind it.

I had been chosen as a stalker-sniper when in training at Folkestone, and I made up my mind to do as much damage as possible with the limited amount of ammunition I had with me. I noticed a German L.M.G. Section had taken cover behind a rock a few hundred yards away, above and to the left of where I had taken up my position. They were firing short bursts at some target on our left flank. I could just make out a blur of light brownish khaki. They were wearing desert-type uniforms and not, as I had expected, the famous field-grey. I fired two rounds at this blob, and the firing ceased for a few seconds. I saw a figure, crawling away from where I had been firing, in the thick undergrowth. I fired and the figure seemed to disappear. Then I saw the glint of sunlight on metal, directly above me and no more than three hundred yards away. I fired five rounds and paused to reload.

I had just reloaded the magazine when I felt as if I had been punched on my right shoulder by a heavyweight boxer, wearing a lump of white hot lead instead of a boxing-glove. My right arm stung as if it had been plunged into a furnace, then suddenly all feeling left it. I tried to pick up my rifle, but my fingers would not work; they opened and shut but they refused to grip. It was a disconcerting experience. I pushed my rifle forward with my left hand and arm, tucking the butt under my left armpit and resting the muzzle on a stone. Thus I fired a final shot, hoping to hit something. I just could not manipulate the bolt. The shock from the blow I had received was making me dizzy and my eyesight was blurred. I noticed that my right shoulder was oozing blood and my battle-dress was a sorry sight.

At this point Dick Garret, my platoon-commander, Sergeant Coxon and Lieutenant Morris, the commander of the platoon immediately to my right, wormed their way towards me and joined me where I lay. Between them they cut open my sleeve, ripped it off, produced one of their own field dressings and bandaged up the wound, thus staunching the flow of blood. This was an act of great courage and one for which I shall always be grateful. They could all have been killed because, in order to put the dressing on, they had to expose themselves to some extent. Anyway they completed the job, ordered me to rest until the numbness left me, and then to make my own way to Battalion H.Q., to report on the position and get proper medical attention.

I lay where I was until the numbness gave way to an intense throbbing, then I looked about me. The company had moved farther down the hill but were still firing with as much determination as before. I put my left hand inside my jacket. Cressida was there, alive and warm; she gently nibbled my fingers. At least we were still together – all was not lost. I slung my rifle over my left shoulder and paused to gain strength and take in the situation. Taking a deep breath I hauled myself to my feet, using my now useless rifle as a lever, and started down the hillside. I had about three-quarters of a mile to go, and I went like a chamois jumping from one cover to another; I soon passed through our own lines and was on my way to H.Q. Then it seemed that every enemy gun was concentrated on me. Bullets were ricocheting off the rocks at my feet as I ran my zig-zagging course down the mountain slope. I felt as if I was about fifty feet high, and it was not a pleasant sensation. I dived into a gulley to recover my breath and get my bearings. As I rose to continue my journey it seemed as if the hillside exploded in my face.

Later, returning to consciousness from a nightmare-haunted delirium, my memory slowly returned through successive whirls of grey mist. It was like awakening after an anaesthetic. I was shivering with cold, soaking wet, but I was alive. As my awareness returned so did the pain; my whole body seemed to be one grinding ache. I managed to roll over on to my left side; my left arm at least still functioned. I now managed to sit up, despite the pain in my chest and right shoulder. My head ached as if from the father and mother of all hangovers, and my right eye was half closed, clotted with dried blood. I found I was still in the gulley where I had taken refuge, and a few yards away flattened against the rock was a piece of metal, a fragment from a rifle grenade. There was a pool of water in a hollow, under a protecting edge of the gulley. I drank down gulp after gulp of its icy goodness, and washed the blood from my face. The cold, clear mountain water did much to counteract the shock of the mauling I had received and brought me to my full senses. For some minutes I rested, my back propped against a heap of earth, a miniature landslide which packed the whole of the lower end of the gully. Here I reclined whilst strength and realisation slowly flooded back to me. My battle-dress was ripped and blackened with drying blood, my shirt seemed to have stuck to my chest, so that it was hard to tell where one began and the other ended. I tried to ease them into some sort of order, but it was too painful.

Of Cressida there was no sign, and a pain more intense than any I had suffered on the battle-field swept through me at the thought of her tragic end, for surely she could never have survived. My sense of loss was absolute. However, I could not stay where I was. I must somehow make my way to B.H.Q. and rejoin my company. After a couple of failures I managed to lever myself partially upright with the help of my rifle; then with my left arm I grasped a root that was hanging over the lip of the gulley and after a struggle hauled myself up. I realised now how much one depends on the use of both arms; my right arm was not only incapacitated, but become a confounded nuisance and seemed to keep getting in the way, as if determined to hold me back and spoil my chances of getting through. I hooked my rifle up by putting my leg through the sling. Concealed as I was behind a tangled wilderness of shrubs there was nothing to indicate that a battle had only a short time before swept down this hillside. The tide had rolled past and left me behind like a stranded starfish. Somewhere far away came the sudden rattle of machine-gun fire, softened and blunted by distance, but it seemed to belong to another world. The sun was hanging like a great tangerine low over the Western Hills, which appeared a soft, silvery purple with the approaching dusk.

I slung my rifle over my left shoulder once more and prepared to move on down the hill. I looked around me; I was alone, alone save for the dead. I felt like the sole survivor of Armageddon and a cold wave of desolation swept over me. As I was about to move on I heard the loud ringing call I knew so well. I spun round and searched the branches of the few stunted trees which that barren rocky hill supported. I saw nothing at first, then, as I peered in the direction from which the call seemed to have come, I thought I saw a reddish brown form moving slightly, low down amongst the branches of an ilex, only fifty yards away. Half hoping, I dragged my unwilling feet through the clutching, tripping vegetation, until I saw what I had in fact expected. It was a bunch of withered leaves, stirred slightly by the evening breeze. But I knew she was there somewhere waiting for me.

I sat down and felt in my trouser pocket until I found a battered cigarette packet which contained two woe-begone but still smokable cigarettes. I had the remnants of a box of matches, and I lit up as my eyes roved the countryside around me. There was a thick bush, a juniper, a few yards in front of me. I thought I saw the lower sprays move slightly, as if a mouse or lizard was passing through them; then I heard the faintest suspicion of a rustle. Despite the pain I almost jumped to my feet and hastened as best I could across the intervening space. I dropped to my knees, and with my one serviceable hand I prised apart the tough black stems. There, crouching in a slight depression of the ground, sat Cressida.

I forced my left hand into the bush and after a struggle she scrambled on to my fist and I carefully drew her out of her hiding-place. Her right wing was hanging motion-less, and she cried out when I tried to examine it. I put her down beside me to recover her composure, and after one or two abortive efforts she half jumped, half flopped on to my knee, which had always been one of her favourite perches. She preened her dishevelled feathers, and hitched her wing back into its proper position. It seemed to be badly bruised but did not appear to be broken. How she had survived at all was beyond me. She must have been resting close to my waist when the rifle grenade had exploded and wounded me, and it must have been my fall that had injured her wing. My tunic being ripped open, she must have scrambled out and made her way to the shelter of the bush. Then when she was feeling better she had dared to call and let me know her whereabouts.

I picked her up, shouldered my rifle and started off once more down the slope, hoping to be able to contact my battalion or what was left of them. By now I was beginning to feel as if the whole thing was happening to some-one else, and I was on the outside looking on; this odd sensation gave place to extreme weariness and I had to rest. As I looked about for suitable cover I nearly fell over an object lying in my path. After some effort I picked it up; it was a Very light pistol. With the pistol beside me I lay down on my back behind a natural screen of large cactus, which hid me from hostile eyes and gave me some sense of security. Cressida settled on a stone nearby and was soon fast asleep. I, too, must have slept or become unconscious, for when I came to my senses the light had almost gone. Cressida was still asleep, standing contentedly on one leg.

As I tried to pull myself together I heard voices close by. I could not determine what language was being spoken; it did not sound German, but it was not English either. Very slowly and painfully I raised my head above the cactus screen; a short distance away, just discernible in the shrinking light, were three tattered forms, shuffling like vultures as they went about their loathsome work. They were a group of the most unsavoury half-caste Arabs who always seem to lurk on the fringes of battle, to

emerge like scavengers to rob the dead of the few possessions they might own. Even as I watched a figure emerged
out of the gloom, a bulging blanket over his shoulder,
and in one hand, held by their laces, a pair of army boots.

Feeling sick at heart and utterly revolted, without
much thought for the ethics of the matter, I raised the
Very light pistol, took some sort of aim and pulled the
trigger. There was a shattering explosion, a blinding
light, followed by inky darkness, also frenzied shouts and
the sound of feet disappearing into the twilit hillside.
When the smoke had cleared the Arabs had gone, leaving
a trail of blankets and loot behind them. I had missed,
but I had done my best. Throwing away the empty and
now useless pistol I picked up Cressida, who appeared
rather less upset emotionally by the recent train of events
than I was. I put her back in my tunic and stumbled on
downwards towards the road. My head was now swimming, and I could hardly see from the fumes in my eyes
and nose. All I wanted was to rejoin my unit and have my
wounds washed. Above all I craved for a cup of real army
tea, with lashings of sugar followed, if possible, by a
decent night's sleep.

Chapter 13

I DIDN'T see the German patrol until I heard a loud, guttural and Teutonic bellow to Halt. I halted sharpish! There seemed to be dozens of them, all around me, and they all seemed to be holding their unpleasantly business-like weapons within an inch of my midriff. They shouted something else, evidently a suggestion that I threw down my rifle and raised my hands on high. Not wishing to have my stomach perforated, I complied as well as I was able, but I indicated that as only one of my arms was functioning properly I hoped that that would do. Their leader, an officer of sorts but of what rank I had no clue, approached me. 'Ah,' said he, 'so you are wounded, hein?' I risked bringing further retribution on my head by pointing out that I had been painfully aware of this fact for some hours, and could in fact hardly stand upright. 'Ach so,' he said, 'for you ze war iss over, and soon you vill go to a German hospital – March!' I marched, flanked by the entire unit, which could have consisted of anything from a platoon to a division so numerous was my bodyguard. I was escorted to what had once been our B.H.Q., pushed inside the dilapidated building and the door was slammed.

When my eyes grew used to the semi-darkness within I saw that the room was full of men in battle-dress. It appeared that almost the whole of the 2/5 Battalion Top Brass were here assembled, who had all been captured shortly before when the H.Q. had been overrun. There was the C.O., the R.S.M. and the Padre; the latter was splendid, collecting blankets from our captors and doing all he could to make the wounded comfortable. The R.S.M., whose name was Henessy, was chatting away about the recent battle in the same way as if it had been a football match. 'Well, sir, at least we winged 'em; they won't forget us in a hurry,' he remarked to the C.O. I was most impressed by this exhibition of nonchalance. I was asked many questions about Cressida. 'Where was she?' 'Had she survived?' 'What was I going to do with her now?' There were a few who strongly advised me to get rid of her; some even suggested I might be shot as a spy and Cressida might be suspected of being a homing-pigeon in disguise.

The awfulness of our position now began to dawn on me, flooding through my mind already partially deadened by pain and fatigue. But I did not have long to think. Suddenly there was the sound of marching feet and Teutonic commands. The door was flung open and the room was full of German soldiers shouting out the one word 'Raus' many times repeated. The effect was like the baying of a pack of savage hounds in full cry, and everyone was herded none too gently on to the roadside where we stood in dejected groups. If there is anything more soul-destroying than the sudden realisation that one is a prisoner of war then I do not wish to experience it. The Padre somehow managed to convey that I was amongst those who had been wounded, and I was escorted to a vehicle that looked like a cross between an ambulance and a single-decker bus. I was pushed towards an empty wooden seat and I flopped down in the corner near the window.

Opposite me was a German soldier, half of whose face was swathed in blood-soaked bandages: we looked at each other but did not speak. There were more shouts outside. The Germans, I was shortly to discover, could apparently do very little without shouting. A uniformed driver climbed into the driver's seat and after a good deal of revving and snorting the machine bounded forward and we were off. Try as I might I could not keep awake. I knew I was slipping into a sort of coma, which I fought hard to overcome, but sheer weariness and a sort of despair combined to produce a powerful anaesthetic. Before I passed out I felt for Cressida where she rested in my blouse. I stroked her head, and she gave my finger a reassuring tweak, which was the last thing I felt before I blacked-out.

When I came to I found that I had slipped forward and was lying with all my weight on the German soldier opposite me. I pulled myself together and returned to a more or less upright position. The soldier, still without speaking, produced a bar of the most delicious chocolate I have ever tasted. Suddenly I realised I was famished, having eaten nothing since the previous evening. I finished the bar and made appropriate noises to express my thanks. My opposite number then produced a packet of cigarettes and offered me one. I noticed they were a well-known American brand, but forbore to comment on this. The ambulance, if that is what it was, lurched and thundered through the night. I slept fitfully until we reached the hospital which was just outside Bizerta. Here the ambulance stopped and we all either climbed out or were carried out.

I was taken under escort to an interview room which again seemed full of Germans, including an interpreter and the M.O. of the hospital, a major in the Medical Corps. I was asked various questions then the order came which I had been dreading ever since my capture. 'Take off your tunic.' I explained that owing to wounds it was impossible, and a number of uniformed figures stepped forward and slit off what was left of my sleeve.

I noticed a window was open in a corner of the room and I made a desperate plan. I put my left hand slowly into my blouse and pressed it gently against Cressida's breast. I felt her grip it with her claws and felt her weight as she climbed on to it. As the medical orderlies began to ease the now sleeveless jacket off I felt for the end of the shortened jesses and took a firm grip with my fingers. After a struggle, like that of a large moth emerging from a very tight chrysalis, the jacket was eased over my head. There in the lamp-light, with her great lambent eyes scrutinising the foe, sat Cressida.

I raised my head and waited for Nemesis to strike. Had there been, as I expected, a bellow of wrath and a concerted rush to take her from me I intended to try to reach the window and cast her off to take her chance. I knew that her wing would soon be strong enough to bear her up; she was in perfect condition, as fat as butter, and if she had had to fast for a few days it would have done her little harm. Besides, with the abundance of grasshoppers, crickets and large beetles that I knew were there for the catching, even a half-witted kestrel should have been able to make some sort of a living, and Cressida was far from being half-witted. But the expected tirade never came.

I glanced at the doctor who was staring at Cressida with an expression of rapture. At last he spoke, '*Ah,*' said he, '*ein turm falke.*' Thus I learned the German name for a kestrel. The atmosphere in that small crowded room relaxed at once. The doctor, through the interpreter, asked me various questions about Cressida, whom he thought must be an official mascot. I told him her whole story. The interpreter's English was not brilliant and my German almost non-existent, but we somehow got the whole thing across. The doctor, it seemed, was a keen amateur naturalist, and he had been a practising falconer before the war; he even produced from his wallet a somewhat faded photograph of a splendid goshawk to prove it. Thus it came about that the only British P.O.W. with a tame kestrel was confronted with probably the only practising falconer in the German Medical Corps in North Africa. Truly the ways of Destiny are strange and wonderful.

The doctor took Cressida on his ungloved left fist, the correct one, and she for her part behaved impeccably: then he put her on the back of a chair and they busied themselves with me. I was a mess, but after the assorted pieces of metal had been extracted from my shoulder and chest, hot water, disinfectant and surgical stitches soon put me to rights. I took Cressida once more on my fist and, escorted by the now friendly and almost respectful bodyguard, I was taken to a ward and shown my bed — a real bed with white sheets and pillow-cases, a bed such as I had not seen since I left Britain nearly three months before. A copy of *Deutscher Arbeiter Zeitung*, or something similar, was produced and spread on the floor between the wall and the back of my bed, and Cressida was installed upon the brass rail at the head after a piece of bandage had been wrapped round it to protect her feet from the chill.

I climbed thankfully into bed, a medical orderly produced some kind of pain-killer or sedative, and after swallowing it I became engulfed in the deepest sleep I have ever experienced. The last thing I remember was the shadow of Cressida, hugely magnified by the flickering lamps, and the great central table in the ward. She seemed to take on the stature of an eagle as she watched over me, surprisingly self-confident and at ease, as I was dragged down into the depths of a coma born of sheer mental and physical exhaustion.

When I surfaced hours later I just could not realise what had happened. I suppose I was still semi-drugged, for the whole situation seemed unreal. However, the truth was soon brought home to me by Cressida, who was by now extremely hungry and waiting for me to do something about it. I looked round the ward, which was full of British soldiers from a number of units, but none unfortunately from the Sherwood Foresters. All had of course been wounded, but none very seriously. A good many were able to walk about and help those who were bed-ridden. When they awoke and saw Cressida perched on my bed rail, some may well have suspected they were still in the throes of a mild delirium. I found I had, in fact, met one or two of my fellow unfortunates in Camberley, or in Liverpool before sailing for Algiers; and these were, to put it mildly, flabbergasted that Cressida håd arrived safely in Africa and even survived the Battle of Sejana. Some perhaps thought I must be some kind of wizard, accompanied by his familiar; if my captors shared this view I was all for encouraging it.

The German O.C., the major I had encountered the previous night, arrived to make his round of inspection. He walked down the row of beds prescribing treatment for the various injuries. When he came to me he discussed my case with his retinue, spoke a few words to me and to Cressida and, just as he was about to move on to the next bed, produced a small tin box and handed it to me. It contained three plump, dead mice. I was lost for words. Cressida's feeding problem was seen to for the day at least. She ate two of the mice in rapid succession, as much at home as if she were sitting on a pollard willow in the middle of Romney Marsh. Soon after her meal she descended from her perch and gave herself a sort of imaginary dust bath on my bed, shuffling about and wagging her tail like an old hen. This also showed that she was in a thoroughly relaxed and contented frame of mind, and ready for anything that might come her way.

My wounds were dealt with efficiently and with a minimum of fuss, and I was able to relax and think over the situation. Obviously the most important things were first to recuperate and then, if possible, to escape. But until my wounds were at least partly healed and I had built up a certain amount of strength, any attempt to break out would be doomed to failure; and then, as a marked man, any further opportunities would be harder to snatch. I had noticed that the hospital itself seemed to have a minimum of security arrangements and only a skeleton staff of armed guards; on the other hand, it stood in a flat plain which, as far as I could see, was a long way from anywhere offering any sort of real cover. Furthermore we knew that the allied lines were no great distance away and after the setback at Sejana there might well be a counter-offensive; and this, in the course of its advance, would overrun the hospital and set us free without any effort on our part. So I lay and pondered hour after hour and listened to all the other patients' tales of woe as to how they came to be there.

At first I was in considerable pain and was given a good deal of morphia; after I had had a shot I could relax and let my mind wander at will. I would dream of my family and friends and what they would think if they could see me now. I thought of the curious situation I was in, for curious it certainly was. Here I was, wounded, a prisoner in the hands of Hitler's Third Reich, probably the most formidable and ruthless enemy with which Britain in all her history had ever had to contend. And yet, here was Cressida, a British-born kestrel, blown by the winds of fortune into a remarkable and probably unique partnership. Transported thousands of miles over the sea, here she was sitting on my bed-rail, and no attempt had been made to sever the link between us. It seemed indeed that all things were possible.

Now excitement was abroad in the hospital; rumours of all sorts could be had for the asking. Far away in the distance could be heard the crump of artillery fire. The Allies were coming — deliverance was at hand. Not so, unfortunately. We were hustled from bed, dressed, much to our amusement and not without indignation, in cast-off uniforms of the Afrika Korps, and whisked off to the local air-strip in the same bus-cum-ambulance in which we had arrived. The doctor said good-bye to us and wished us well. I shall always remember him with gratitude and I hope he survived the war.

Cressida was concealed in my Wehrmacht uniform tunic as we boarded the J.U.52 transport planes lined up waiting for us. The prospect of crossing the Mediterranean in these lumbering monsters, each clearly marked with the Iron Cross, was not alluring, being targets for the first Spitfire or Hurricane that came that way. However, we were lucky, and after an uneventful but decidedly bumpy flight we landed at Palermo safely. Here we were immediately surrounded by a herd of scruffy and vociferous Italian soldiers, all determined to make up in noise what they lacked in inches. It soon became obvious that we had been handed over to their custody. I personally found it hard to forgive the Germans for this, because Italians eat birds irrespective of species! I looked at the soldiers, who seemed to be inspecting us as if we were so much beef on the hoof. I deemed Cressida would have been a match for most of them; but it did not come to a combat of that sort. Instead we were herded into another ambulance and driven to a hospital, a civilian one this time on the outskirts of Palermo.

Here we thankfully climbed into beds again. Many of us were still suffering a good deal, and fever ridden. This time we were in the hands of a religious order, and the Sisters of Mercy were all that their name implied. Their habits were similar to those worn by nuns of many Orders, but the coifs with their wide upturned brims were distinctive and attractive, reminiscent of Madonna lilies. The ward in which I was now confined was attractive and sunny, looking out on to a large courtyard beyond which arose a rather exciting-looking ruin. The ward itself was under the guardianship of an Italian corporal, who proved a most affable and co-operative fellow. His chief complaint seemed to be that he, a citizen of Florence, should be stranded here amongst such barbarians as these Sicilians, who apparently did not even speak the same language.

I took him into my confidence and introduced him to Cressida, with the same result as in the German hospital. No one raised any objection after the initial shock had worn off. I explained that she needed fresh meat daily and he enlisted the help of one of the Sisters of Mercy. The result was that every day a substantial portion of raw meat duly arrived for Cressida, who throve accordingly. In fact, about the only Italian words I ever learned were *carne cruda*, raw meat; *uccello*, meaning a bird; and *falcone*.

What did rather surprise me was that none of my enforced hosts raised the subject of hygiene. In this case a piece of paper was spread on the broad white window-ledge behind my bed. One of my boots was provided for a perch, proving a satisfactory substitute for a rock, and that was that. My neighbour in the next bed was a pleasant and accommodating young man from, I think, the Hampshire Regiment. He and I used to hold long conversations far into the night on a variety of subjects, ranging from natural history and travel to religion and politics; we also talked about the books we both missed, as of course no literature was provided for us. We did, however, acquire a tattered copy of a book called *The Ragged Trousered Philanthropists*, which was exceedingly heavy going, and of which I can remember not one single word.

In the late afternoon, but while the sun was still high in the sky, a flock of large bats used to issue forth from the ruins opposite and provide me with hours of entertainment as they skimmed and swerved about the deserted courtyard. I did not know what species they might be, but I now think that they must have been mouse-eared bats, which are as big as, or even bigger than, the British noctule, and are a widely distributed continental species. Cressida used to spend hours sunbathing in the strong Sicilian sunlight. Although the window was open, she made no attempt to leave the room and showed little interest in exploring the outside world which, knowing the avicidal tendencies of the natives, was probably just as well for her.

I enjoyed my sojourn in the hospital, and have only praise for the treatment I received there. Above all it was a joy just to lie warm and relaxed, with no responsibility other than Cressida, and to let the war run its course without me. But like all good things this splendid period of inactivity had to come to an end. My wounds had healed up and the time had come to move on. When a batch of prisoners had recovered sufficiently and there were enough to make it worth while, we were rounded up and piled once more into trucks. We were then driven through the streets of Palermo, narrow and smelly and crowded with people who appeared to be anything but hostile towards the *Inglese*. The truck, driven with the usual southern Italian frenzy and an apparent complete disregard for safety, climbed up the winding Sicilian roads and approached the mountains as dusk came. We soon reached our destination, which proved to be Camp P.G. 98.

The accommodation consisted of a number of large tents laid out on natural terraces in the foothills of the central Sicilian mountains. The beds, double- or treble-tiered wooden bunks, were appalling; we had insufficient blankets, and the food situation was lamentable to say the least. The only consolation, which hardly made up for the shortcomings, was the magnificent scenery. When we arrived, although it was April, there was still snow on the ground; the change of temperature after the warmth and comfort of the hospital, together with the abysmal rations we received, were more lowering to our morale than anything that had happened to us since our capture.

Here I knew for the first time in my life what it is like to be permanently hungry. Our daily rations consisted of a small bread roll and a cupful of watery soup which, if we were lucky, contained a few sprigs of what looked like and probably was chickweed. Not being a canary this diet was not to my liking. At seven each morning, after shivering our way through the night, we were greeted with a cauldron of ersatz black coffee of an almost unbelievable nastiness. Life, as can be imagined, was anything but jolly.

Cressida, however, fared better, better in fact than at any time since leaving Algeria. The tents and their environs were infested with mice, the grassy slopes outside held their quota of voles, and Cressida lost no time in taking advantage of this. She sometimes caught three or four in the course of an afternoon. I would sit in the sunlight outside the tent with Cress on my knee, and she became an expert in taking any vole or mouse that was unwise enough to leave its sanctuary without first taking a good look round. The camp was big enough for her to take all the exercise she needed without approaching the wire, which was bristling with machine-guns, rifles, and goodness knows what else. The Italian guards were notoriously trigger-happy, with a habit of blasting away on the least provocation; and at this particular time they were even more edgy than usual because they were expecting an Allied invasion and they had, we suspected, been charged with our safe custody on pain of death or worse by their so-called allies. By now the German forces in Tunisia were more or less at the point of collapse.

Our camp held representatives of every nation that could even vaguely be associated with the Allied cause. Apart from British, Americans, South Africans, Free French, and many others, were hordes of Arabs of the type I had last encountered skulking on the battle-field of Sejana. What they were doing here was anyone's guess, but as they hardly came into the category of bona fide prisoners of war one can only suppose that the Germans had a more subtle sense of humour than they were usually credited with. Here, anyway, these Arabs were a confounded nuisance and they ate the meagre rations that we could ill afford to share.

I had not been long at this camp when I, together with most of the other inmates, went down with a particularly virulent form of dysentery which, aided by our weakness and by virtual starvation, reduced us to the state of zombies. We hardly had sufficient energy to move to the latrines, and at one period many of us took our blankets and lay down within a few yards of them, so as to be near when nature called, which she did about every ten minutes. We were eventually inoculated against this revolting complaint, but the Italian idea of hygiene was to say the least primitive. The medical orderly, whose job it was to inject us, used the same needle over and over again without sterilising it, just wiping off the blood on his grimy overall; once he dropped the syringe on the filthy floor of the hut which was used as an M.I. room, picked it up and wiping it on his overall carried on as before. None the less most of us survived this outbreak, but for quite a long period I was so weak that I could not even take Cressida out to catch her mice.

At first I was in a state of semi-consciousness and had to leave her to her own devices; in spite of this she refused to desert me, remaining within the compound, catching such small rodents as came her way and returning to my tent at dusk to roost on my bed. Many a time, as I lay shivering and almost desperate with hunger, the sight of her perched within a few inches of my head did more to keep up my morale than anything, and some of my comrades told me they felt much the same. Of course the Italian camp staff knew of her presence and were rather nonplussed about it. Cressida, for her part, had for the first time since our partnership become distinctly aggressive. Whether she sensed that the Italians were our enemies, or whether she sensed that they were nervous of her, I cannot say. Whatever it was, if they came too close or gesticulated too wildly she would mantle ferociously and go for them striking with her feet and shrieking with rage. This was both embarrassing and unwise because, for all her courage, she could not have survived a direct hit from a Baretti bullet. I often wondered what I would have done if one of the guards had in fact threatened her life. I like to think that I would have done her credit. Luckily, though, it never came to that. Cressida undoubtedly bore a charmed life.

Chapter 14

AT about this time I met Tom Costang. Tom was in my
regiment but belonged to another company. He had been
a promising pilot and had volunteered for the Airborne
Division, where he had trained as a 'Tug Pilot.' In other
words it would have been his job to pilot planes that
towed the gliders to their destination before an airborne
invasion. Tom had passed out well but unfortunately,
being an Irishman of an exceptionally volatile temperament, he had celebrated his success, which incidentally
had coincided with his birthday, by taking up a trainer
plane without the formality of asking permission. Having
celebrated too well the result was that he crashed the
plane, thus finishing up as a private in the 2/5 Sherwood
Foresters.

Tom was not only a trained pilot but, together with great plausibility and the proverbial wit of the Irish, he proved to be a thief of almost professional standards. This made him indeed a friend worth having. His first notable success was to rob the Italian ration store of a prodigious cheese intended for the consumption of our hosts. He and I and a few others enjoyed this enormously, the more so as we heard howls of frustrated rage coming from the quarters of our custodians. A snap search was mounted and produced nothing, not even a piece of rind. He surpassed this later by breaking into the wine store, which for some reason was, like the cook-house, confined within the perimeter of the camp. He stole enough bottles of the delicious local wine to make us, the lucky participants, almost completely blotto. Another search was instituted and again nothing was found. This called for some pretty clever acting, as it is far from easy to pretend to be stone cold sober when one can hardly stand. Luckily this was before the advent of the breathalyser.

We often talked about the possibility of escape, but at this time we were still far too weak physically to be able to stand up to the rigours that we knew such a venture would entail. Then came a consignment of Red Cross parcels. These put an entirely different complexion on matters, and I am convinced that had it not been for these life-giving parcels few of us would have survived. Each of these had to be shared between four, so it was some time before we could think of anything much except our stomachs.

Spring had now come to Sicily; even here in this half life that we were living we felt the stirrings, faint though they were. Even in the prison camp nature was at work; amongst the grass suddenly appeared drifts of wild narcissi, and from clefts in the rocky soil, where they had been hibernating, came the wall lizards, to bask in the first early strengthening of the sun's rays. Once a green lizard, well over a foot in length, emerged sleepily to enjoy the warmth of the granite slab beneath which he had his den. The camp became a lepidopterist's paradise, Black-veined and Bath whites, butterflies virtually unknown in Britain, were here abundant rising like belated snowflakes at every step. Swallowtails, in a galaxy of blues, appeared as if by magic, floating like animated blossoms above the carpet of gentians, grape hyacinths and violets. At night hawk moths of several species came to hover over the multi-coloured convolvuli.

With the quickening of my blood came once more a desire to escape and to enjoy the spring untrammelled. Cressida, too, began to show reaction to the changing season. She would sit atop some prominent outcrop of rock, where she could see far down into the valley below. From time to time she would fan her tail, raise the feathers on her nape and give vent to her loud, clear, ringing call. When spoken to by me or any of her particular friends, she would bow her head, raise her expanded tail and click with a curious metallic sound like two pebbles striking against each other. She was in immaculate plumage and at the peak of condition.

One day, when I was walking the circumference of the compound with Cressida on my fist, she suddenly hurled herself off it and dashed at a wall lizard which was baking on a warm slab of rock. The lizard saw her coming and raced for his hole, his legs carrying him at incredible speed, but Cressida with the advantage of height, after a short but exciting chase, grabbed him just before he dived into shelter. She did not, as one might have expected, make the mistake of grabbing the tail which would have come off in her foot; instead she took him by the head and carried him to a convenient flat-topped granite rock, a perfect dining-table. He was dead almost as soon as she hit him and she ate him tail and all, looking extremely self-satisfied about the whole performance.

Tom and I used to sit for hours on a bank at the highest part in the compound and talk, and our conversation was about two things, food and the possibility of escape. To us, as we sat there one afternoon smoking the last of our Red Cross cigarettes, came three American soldiers, Les, Joe and Hank, all volunteers who had crossed into Canada at the outbreak of war when it appeared that the U.S.A. was going to remain neutral. They had joined the Canadian Army but, on the entry of the U.S.A. after Pearl Harbour, they had somehow arranged a transfer back into their own army. They had, like myself, been captured in the last desperate push of the Germans in their final endeavour to maintain their foothold.

We chatted for some time before we broached the subject that was uppermost in all our minds. We had all, long ago, decided that the hospitality we were receiving was not of the standard to which we were accustomed, and we made up our minds there and then to do what we could to remedy the situation. We planned to cut the wire, take to the hills and work our way southward until we came to a small fishing village on the coast. Here we hoped to steal a boat and sail either to Malta or to a part of Africa which we knew to be in Allied hands. To bring this plan to a successful conclusion we needed assistance and equipment.

It happened that in the camp was an American top-sergeant, a rank that was new to me, but which I assume to be more or less the equivalent of the British regimental-sergeant-major. Toppy, as he was called, proved to be a first-class friend and fellow-conspirator. We suggested that he should come with us on our adventure, but he explained, quite rightly, I think, that with his rank he was in a position of considerable authority even though himself a captive. He considered that he could be of more help to his compatriots by remaining in the camp, doing his best to mediate with the enemy, and thus ensure that such things as the Geneva Convention were adhered to. Although he had decided not to accompany us he did all in his power to help us in other ways. He owned a magnificent and most expensive chronometer and a certain amount of lira, both of which he had somehow managed to retain after capture. These he made over to us. He was also no mean cartographer and we spent long hours preparing a map of Sicily. As none of us had ever been there before, we could rely only on the geography we had learned in our schooldays, so our task was not an easy one.

We needed food for our journey, and decided to wait until we had hoarded a supply of Red Cross rations, which we buried in a box in a place known only to the six of us. We agreed that the fewer people who knew about our project the better, as there were spies planted by the enemy posing as P.O.W.s; and far more unpleasant, traitors in our own ranks were not unknown. We took only one more ally into our confidence, Guido, who was an American citizen of Italian descent. Although he spoke Italian as his mother tongue, he was a loyal American. He was a great help to us, his job being to get all the information he could about troop movements, arrangements regarding guard changing and anything he could glean of the Italian routine. Tom, our 'burglar,' was given the most important but unenviable job of all, he had to steal the wire-cutters and later cut the wire.

We chose 14th May for The Day when we were to make our bid for freedom. This, as it happened, was my birthday, but, what was much more important, it was also some special Saint's Day, and we knew from previous experience that there would be great local celebrations and a large number of our foes would be so drunk that they would be unlikely to hit us, even if they had not mislaid their weapons. Meanwhile there was much to be done. Tom first located the wire-cutters. On some pretext or other he managed to bribe or flatter his way into the camp stores, and his quick eyes speedily took in the layout. He also discovered a large screwdriver which he promptly purloined, so that our entrance into the storeroom at the right time was now assured.

The days passed and excitement grew. It was hard not to talk to our friends and tent mates of what we had in mind, but we dared not do so. The time of waiting was of almost unbearable suspense. We had much at stake. On the one hand, if we succeeded, there was the tantalising lure of freedom and all that meant to us; on the other hand, if we failed, possibly death, or years of the sort of life-in-death that we had been leading in the prison camp. It was worth the risk.

On the morning of 13th May we all met at our appointed rendezvous to make our final plans. Tom would have to steal the wire-cutters during the time the attention of the guards was directed elsewhere. It was arranged that someone, not actually a member of the escape party but chosen for his histrionic ability, should go suddenly and vociferously mad, or have an acute attack of epilepsy. This in itself presented problems, because if the part was too well acted there was always the chance that the joke might misfire and the poor devil find himself in an Italian lunatic asylum, a grim prospect. The wire-cutters had to be stolen during daylight, because anyone moving about after dark was liable to be shot without the least compunction. Zero hour was to be at 1.30 on the morning of the 14th.

At about 11.30 a.m. on the 13th bedlam suddenly broke out, shrieks and yells were heard from one of the adjacent huts, and guards could be seen converging on it, like bees to a honeypot. Our actor was doing his part well. Tom took his screwdriver and sauntered casually in the direction of the store, whilst Guido, the linguist, engaged the armed guard, who was nominally in charge of it, in earnest conversation regarding the delights of life in the U.S.A. and the chances of emigrating there after the war. The store was out of sight behind a fold in the ground, but a stooge had been posted to give warning of any untoward enemy activity. Tom reappeared, moving swiftly in the direction of his tent. I thought I detected a slight bulge beneath his camouflaged parachute jacket. As he passed below us, he glanced up and nodded his head. Phase No. 1 was successfully completed. One at a time we returned to the tent where Tom had already buried the wire-cutters beside the rations.

The rest of that day we lay idling in the long grass outside the hut, nibbling chocolate and waiting. Dusk came and the usual evening roll-call. We retired to our bunks to rest and think, though sleep for any of us was out of the question. I lay on my pack watching Cressida, who was lazily preening herself; her crop was distended with a big fat vole that she had eaten that day. Good! She would not need a meal for at least twenty-four hours. Each of the conspirators had been given a haversack, contributed by the top-sergeant who had tactfully let it be known that something was afoot, but without going into too many details. My haversack already contained three dead lizards and the small tin given to me by the German doctor, crammed with locusts. These were Cressida's emergency rations. I looked at her contentedly picking her toes and wished I could explain what lay before her. I had already made a sort of compartment inside my old Wehrmacht jacket, where I hoped she would be safe until we were well clear of the camp.

At 23.30 hours we gathered in the tent beneath which the rations and wire-cutters were buried. Tom disinterred the things we needed and rations were distributed. Each haversack contained three bars of Red Cross chocolate, three Italian bread rolls, one box of Canadian Red Cross raisins, two tins of sardines, a tin of Spam, and last but by no means least twenty cigarettes and a box of matches. This just about filled the pack. Tom had the chronometer and Les the maps. It was intended that if any of the party were killed or recaptured the others would push on, either together or, if necessary, each making his own individual effort.

As we had hoped and anticipated some of the guards

were obviously befuddled with much wine drinking, but we did not of course know whether this applied to those actually manning the machine-gun posts. By careful observation over a long period we had discovered that there was a part of the wire which the sweeping searchlights just failed to illuminate and which by a merciful providence appeared to be between the beats of the two sentries who, we decided, were far from conscientious on their patrols. No escapes had been attempted from this camp apparently and the staff was therefore not as suspicious as one might expect.

At 01.00 hours, thirty minutes before Zero, I picked up Cressida from her roosting-place and popped her into my jacket, where she settled down at once. Slinging my pack over my shoulder I crept out into the alley between the two tents where the break-out was to take place. We were all there; Tom, Les, Hank, and Joe Croaty, and Guido to keep watch and speed us on our way. We crawled into the warm darkness. My palms were sticky and my mouth parched. Cressida snuggled up against my chest. Tom looked at his watch, 1.20; he crouched down and slid forward, moving like a Red Indian. The moonlight glinted on the metal wire-cutters in his hand. We had all covered our boots with rags to muffle the sound of our studs on stones.

Zero Hour, 1.30 a.m. Tom had reached the first apron of wire; we heard the grating and clicking as he started cutting, but we saw only his feet as we lay in line behind him. After what seemed an aeon of time we heard a rasping, slithering sound, like that made by a large snake passing over rough ground. Tom's feet were disappearing. He had cut a hole in the first apron, and now we heard faintly the dry grinding and snap as the cutters went to work upon the main obstruction. The sentry, out of sight in his box only a few yards to our left and twenty feet above us, broke into the refrain of 'O Sole Mio,' and how we blessed him for it. Tom was grunting and shuffling like a foraging hedgehog, but each muffled snap meant that we were just that much nearer to freedom. Suddenly Tom was not there. In a silent half-crouching run he had cleared the white ribbon of road and plunged into the cover of the vineyard below. Les followed, then Hank, and I came fourth; one moment I was crouching, poised like a hunting leopard, the next, without apparently any physical effort, I was lying panting beside Hank, half buried in the welcoming tendrils of the infant vines. Seconds later a black bulk hurled itself almost on top of me; it was Joe. We were out! We had made it!

We had decided to make for the hills and, after finding a sheltering cave of which we hoped there were many, to make further plans when we saw what the situation was like and what the opposition appeared to be doing about it. We set off in single file at as brisk a pace as we could muster, although we were hampered by our lack of physical fitness and our almost total lack of knowledge regarding the terrain we were crossing. Upon one thing, however, we were determined — we would put as much distance between us and our late hosts as possible in the few hours of darkness we had left. We knew that at the dawn roll-call our absence would be noted and all hell would be let loose.

We travelled along the upper terrace of the vineyard, which lay just below and out of reach of the camp lights. Even the mobile searchlights could hardly pick us out at that angle. We came at last to where the vineyard was bounded by a high wall, surmounted with bits of jagged glass as a deterrent to would-be intruders. Tom took off his parachute jacket and slung it across the wall; Les added his American combat jacket, and thus padded against the worst of its fangs we heaved, pushed and grunted our way over, to land in a narrow, dusty, cobbled lane. Another wall, unprotected by glass, followed and then we were out on the lower slopes of the mountain. The cool night breeze, spiced with the tang of snow, came to urge us onwards and upwards. Our progress was hindered by great outcrops of quartz and granite that had to be skirted; razor-sharp rocks lay in wait to rip our already pathetically thin boots to ribbons, and we well knew that, if lamed, we would be at the mercy of our pursuers. We were, however, lucky in one thing; the Italians, unlike the Germans, did not use tracker dogs. We blessed them for this oversight.

We came to a natural shelter beneath a huge rock slab, that appeared to be balanced precariously on two great rounded boulders; it looked as if a puff of wind would bring it crashing down upon us, but it may well have rested thus for centuries. Here we each smoked a cigarette, our first in freedom for nearly three months. We shook hands without speaking before pressing on farther into the mountains, which were now raising their great heads on all sides as we climbed ever higher into their welcoming protection.

Eventually we decided that we had travelled far enough for the first leg of our journey, besides which we were physically beyond any further effort. Caves and cavities of all sizes were plentiful; we chose one, a long narrow tunnel whose mouth was almost hidden by a tangled growth of vegetation, and which gave us a superb, panoramic view of the countryside we had just crossed. We could even see a yellow blur, which we knew to be the camp where, ignorant of the drama that had so recently taken place, slumbered the prisoners, whose numbers had been reduced by just five men and a kestrel.

We, from our cave mouth high above the sleeping valley, looked out upon what we had left behind us. I, for one, experienced a sensation such as I have never felt since: thankfulness, and a sense of triumph for what we had accomplished, combined with a curious lofty detachment from the world so far below us. Whatever might happen on the morrow at least we had done our best and no one could take this moment from us. I felt for Cressida, who climbed sleepily on to my fist; not a feather was out of place, her temper quite unruffled as she stepped quietly on to a ledge on the rock within the cavern and settled down to sleep, as if this had been the most ordinary day of her life. We collected piles of dry grass and ferns for our bedding and settled down to spend the remainder of the dark hours at rest, if not in sleep. We had found a tiny trickle of water, running down the wall of the cave to the floor, where it had formed a pool large enough to wash in, the trickle being just sufficient for us to quench our burning thirsts. We smoked cigarettes and munched chocolate. Let to-morrow take care of itself; at least for the moment we were free.

I woke to the sound of distant machine-gun fire. We all rolled out of our respective piles of grass and crowded at the cave mouth. There was a small plateau immediately to the front of us and, as we gazed out across the valley, dawn was filling the mountainside with mist. Glimpsed between the white curtains arising from the valley floor far below us, we could just locate the area of our recent incarceration. The firing grew more intense. 'What the hell are these goddam Germans up to?' inquired one of the Americans. The ghastly thought occurred to us that perhaps the Italians, having discovered our absence, were shooting down the other prisoners as a form of retaliation. Then the truth dawned on us. Running true to form, they were venting their frustration and wrath by firing volley after volley at the inoffensive mountains; in the hope, one can only assume, that this would terrify us into returning voluntarily to captivity, or perhaps to discourage others from making a similar attempt.

We were in a splendid position; we could see for miles on three sides and our rear was guarded by range after range of savage mountains, stretching far into the interior. We decided to rest that day so as to let the hue and cry die down, and for someone to reconnoitre our future route before dusk. We decided to post a sentry with the usual hours of duty, two on and four off, just in case the opposition should mount a full-scale search of what must have seemed to them the obvious escape route. When my turn on guard came I sat with my back propped against a sun-warmed boulder, at a point where I could see the slightest sign of anything suspicious for miles around. Cressida was sitting on another boulder a few yards off, eating one of the lizards I had brought and completely unperturbed by the events of the last few hours. After finishing her lizard she fluffed herself out until she appeared nearly twice her normal size and had a combined sun and dust bath, shuffling about all over her boulder, picking up minute bits of stone in her beak and snatching at them with her brilliant yellow feet; pouncing playfully on the flies, which were present even at that altitude, and finally stretching out both her wings and tail and half closing her eyes as she revelled in the life-giving warmth. I sat in my eyrie, musing about the past and wondering what on earth the future had in store for us all.

Suddenly I noticed Cressida alert once more, staring intently at something on the mountain wall behind us; a small grey bird appeared, fluttering like a butterfly about the crevices and clinging to the lichen-covered rocks, its crimson wings half open, its long beak questing for tiny insects. My duty forgotten, I clambered to my feet and approached to within a few yards of this exquisite creature, which seemed suspended by an invisible thread from the cliff-top. Eventually satisfied, it let itself fall, to be caught by a gust of wind and carried out of sight round a fold in the mountain-side. It was my one and only glimpse of a wall creeper.

It occurred to us that the camp authorities might, after a nominal search, relax to some extent and hope that we would either be starved into giving ourselves up or blunder into a road block or ambush. However, with our limited rations, we could not lie up where we were for very long, and we were by no means certain what the attitude of the civilian population would be towards us. One thing was quite clear; we would soon find out, for we would have to buy or steal food to replenish our fast-diminishing supplies. Meanwhile we determined to enjoy our freedom. That night and all the next day we rested, slowly regaining our strength. Then, at dusk, we ate our final meal and decided to make a forced march, hurrying as fast as we could southward. Cressida had finished her grasshoppers, and so for her sake too we would have to do something to improve our position.

As the moon rose we buried the evidence of our temporary occupation, and left the cave that had proved so helpful an ally. Like a robber band we stole silently out and away, moving much faster than on the previous journey. We still kept to the foothills, because we wanted

to get as far from the camp as we could before making our first contact with civilisation. Sicily is an essentially mountainous country, ideal for any last stand, and I did not envy the Allies the task of winkling out a stubborn enemy from this complex of natural fortifications.

One of our major weaknesses was that we had no idea of the size of the isle, our map being of the most primitive description. However, we knew that if we kept on walking we would reach the coast eventually. We walked all that night and made good progress. At times it seemed that we five were the only human beings left. Any isolated farmhouses or hamlets that we might have passed were now far below us, and we appeared to have lost all contact with the twentieth century. Surely, I thought, Robin Hood and his men must have felt as we did, with every man's hand against them. I hoped that I, a modern Sherwood Forester, would do them credit.

Before dawn began to break we sought for another shelter. This was also a cave, higher and wider than the other. It did not penetrate so deeply into the hillside, but it would serve its purpose – indeed, it had to. Once more we made our couches of dried grass and leaves and ate a frugal meal of sardines and stale Italian bread. Again we found an excellent water supply; a steel-grey torrent, sharp with the bite of melting ice from the high peaks, was rushing down a sheer wall of rock a hundred yards away. The rocks were thick with soft, green moss, which we found served admirably as sponges to bathe our hands and faces. Then, hunger and thirst temporarily at bay, we rolled on to our grassy beds and slept deeply, waking hours later to the unexpected and far from welcome sound of a cock crowing.

Furtively we peered from our shelter, alert as foxes at the mouth of their den. Away below us, but at no great distance, was a white-walled farmhouse. As we watched, two figures emerged and started working in the garden outside. They appeared to be an elderly man and his wife, but what was of more concern to us was who else might be living or billeted there. The small farmstead seemed to be completely isolated, but we guessed it must be part of a community, for Italian country folk are not noted for living a great distance from their kith and kin. We saw no signs of telephone wires, and indeed it was most unlikely that Sicilian peasants of those days would have had a telephone. We formed our plan. We would wait and see if anyone visited the house and then, if no one else emerged, we would descend upon them and coerce them into selling anything edible that might be available. The sight of small bantam-like fowls scratching away in the fields below made our mouths water. Fowls meant eggs, roast chicken and any number of delicious dishes.

We decided that four of us would invade the farmhouse whilst the fifth kept watch from above. We drew lots and Joe was the unlucky one. We waited till late afternoon, and then decided to get on with it. The old couple, who had been working around the house all day, had now disappeared within. No one else had shown up, and there was no apparent sign of any enemy troops, German or Italian. We spread out and covered the quarter of a mile to the farm at a fast jog-trot. On reaching the house Les went round to the back, while Tom, Hank and I knocked loudly on the front door. After an interval that seemed interminable footsteps could be heard shuffling down the passage. The door was opened slightly and a high-pitched voice broke into a babble of hysterical and totally unintelligible Italian. We pushed our way in and were confronted by an elderly peasant, unshaven and smelling strongly of garlic and cheese. He appeared to be paralysed with fright, poor old boy, at the sight of us, and indeed we must have appeared a desperate crew of ruffians. He seemed unable to make out whether we were deserters from the German Army or members of the local Mafia intent on loot, rape or murder. When we managed somehow by dint of mime, gesticulation and a mixture of

English, bad French, and worse German, to explain who we were, the tension relaxed; the old man produced wine glasses and sat us down at a long table, covered with fruit and vegetables. He introduced his wife who had been skulking in the passage, too timid to enter.

This particular couple, it seemed, were not over fond of their German allies, and they did not care much for the peninsular Italians either. They insisted we drank with them and that we drank to a speedy Allied victory. We drank glass after glass of excellent Sicilian wine; we drank so much and were so out of practice that we almost forgot the reason for our somewhat precipitate entry into the lives of these simple people. We produced pocketfuls of lira and suggested that it was changed into *mangiani*. The old man and his wife could hardly have been more accommodating. From a recess in the wall the woman produced an attractive china dish full of small, but delicious-looking, brown eggs. We filled our jacket pockets with them, a large loaf apiece, and a huge wedge of cheese. Finally, as a *pièce de résistance*, we were presented with a pullet of a breed unknown to me but which must, I think, have been an Ancona. At first our host and hostess were unwilling to accept payment, but we insisted and filled their hands with lira.

The old peasants somehow made it clear that from now on we were leaving the mountains and that the Germans were both numerous and active in the district. We thanked them both for their kindness and, after a final glass of wine, returned to the cave as fast as the wine would allow; to the anxious Joe, who demanded where his share of the wine was, and to Cressida who had remained to keep Joe company. The first thing I did was to remove a leg from the pullet and give it to Cressida, who had her first meal of fresh meat since our escape.

We decided to withdraw to another hide-out for the rest of our stay in the area; not that we distrusted our Sicilian hosts but we could not be too careful. We found a mountain-side literally pock-marked with caves, and in one of these we went to ground with our spoils. Joe cooked the chicken in the way beloved of Boy Scouts and pioneers, on a home-made spit. We had overlooked one thing in our excitement, and soon we were spluttering and staggering to the entrance, our eyes watering from the smoke. However, we were able to retrieve our chicken, which we enjoyed enormously. Cressida had wisely decided to stay outside, and when she had finished I carefully stowed away the little that was left.

When I had been living in the Lake District I met a number of men whose whole lives seemed to revolve around their whippets or coursing greyhounds, and amongst the lore I had assimilated was one tip that apparently never failed. Before a race or course, I was told, each dog was given a raw egg broken, for some strange reason, against the animal's teeth. This apparently gave it the necessary stamina. This flashed through my mind now and I did likewise, though I drew the line at the tooth-tapping bit. I swallowed two eggs in rapid succession and found they were not as unpleasant as I had expected. Anyway, I now felt ready to cope with any emergency.

We had toyed with the idea of buying or stealing civilian clothes so that we could travel in daylight and move freely with the local population; but half-remembered stories of P.O.W.s in the last war being shot as spies for doing just that deterred us. Also there was the fact that Tom and I, being six foot tall, would certainly have called for some comment amongst the comparatively diminutive Sicilians.

We slept and rested until nightfall and then once more stole forth to continue our journey to the south. The situation was now becoming much more difficult. Although the country was still hilly we were leaving the mountains behind, and although we knew that every mile we travelled was taking us nearer our goal we knew too that our journey would become more dangerous as we entered the populated, agricultural district. We spread out to some extent, but we dared not leave too much space between us lest we lost touch in the darkness.

We came to a road, the road to Ragusa, and decided to take risks for the sake of speed, as it was leading in the direction we wanted to go. We had travelled for perhaps half a mile when we heard the distant rumble of approaching motor transport. We leaped up the rocky bank which rose almost vertically above the dusty, flint-strewn road. Hardly had we flattened ourselves behind such cover as the sparse vegetation afforded than a column of German trucks, flanked by motor cyclists and filled with singing and shouting troops, came round the corner. Such was the height of these vehicles, which had machine-guns mounted in the back, that their crews must have passed within a few feet of where we crouched like a covey of scared partridges.

When they had gone we had a cigarette each to help restore our equanimity. It was a nasty moment, and reminded us just how vulnerable we were. I know that I would have been happy to have felt the comforting weight of a rifle over my shoulder. For us it was now a case of speed above all else, and so we trudged on all through the night. No longer could we expect the friendly shelter of a cave to hide us during the daylight hours. We passed a cluster of hovels, where dogs barked at us, and soon found ourselves in a citrus grove; here at least we could stave off our thirst with pocketfuls of stolen fruit.

We were rapidly descending towards the coastal flats. When day came and we had as yet found no shelter we felt as conspicuous as five figures in an Antarctic landscape, except that there we would have had nothing more sinister to contend with than the penguins. The only advantage here was that the countryside seemed to be criss-crossed with goat trails; sticking to these we made good progress, as we dropped swiftly from ledge to ledge. Full morning light found us still on the move and not a refuge did we find.

We passed an attractive cottage that had a small shrine let into the wall. We paused, half intending to seek out some barn or outbuilding in which we could hide. Our minds were made up for us when the owner, a shifty and unkempt peasant, came round the corner and shouted something that appeared to be anything but a welcome. We felt like stopping and teaching him better manners, but decided against it. We then retraced our steps and made a detour, sweeping round in a wide arc, and plunged into one of the ever-present vineyards, limping onwards as fast as our tired feet would carry us. At the far end, in the angle where two boundary walls met, stood a ramshackle hut; this was probably used as a shelter for the vineyard workers at the height of the grape harvest, but was now in dire need of repair. However, it would serve; we dived into its inadequate cover and lay down to rest and think.

Our feet by now were badly blistered; thankfully we took off our boots, and the remains of our socks, and wrapped our burning, aching feet in freshly-picked vine leaves, which proved both soothing and refreshing. We ate some cheese and sucked tangerines until we felt a bit more cheerful; but for the first time since our escape we felt the fear of the hunted creeping over us. We did not speak much, but longed for darkness and the obscurity it brought. I had Cressida on my fist and was feeding her with the remains of the chicken leg, when somewhere in the distance we heard faintly the barking of dogs.

Most of the farms in Sicily had watch-dogs, and poor, dejected, underfed beasts they were. We didn't take much notice, until we suddenly realised that the sound was drawing closer and closer; suddenly it stopped and the silence was more unnerving still. Then we saw them. Three great grey shapes were loping towards us at a frightening speed, now lost to sight in a fold of the ground, now appearing once more. Wolves? Surely not in Sicily, and in any case they would hardly attack in daylight in early summer. These were no wolves, but Alsatians, and they knew their job only too well. Over the skyline came a line of German troops, fully armed and shouting encouragement to their sinister pack.

Chapter 15

I HAD just enough foresight to replace Cressida in my tunic as the first Alsatian, now only yards away, slid to a halt barking even more frenziedly and, as if to add insult to injury, vigorously wagging its great flag of a tail. It was joined seconds later by its two companions who, I was glad to see, remained like the first at a respectful distance. So this was what the hunted stag, brought at last to bay, must feel. Hank, Joe and Les made some appropriate remarks in purest Brooklynese, but the normally irrepressible Tom said nothing and I was more or less numb from exhaustion and the sudden turn of events.

We did not have much time to consider our predicament. In an instant we were almost overwhelmed by the enemy, who swept down and surrounded us, all the while keeping up a yelping volume of incomprehensible orders and counter-orders. The three dogs, now leashed, eyed us hungrily. Even at that moment I could not help admiring their remarkable discipline; they seemed twice as large and three times as ferocious as their English relatives. To the now familiar chorus of *Raus! Raus!* we were pushed and prodded along the road we had so recently travelled in freedom.

We passed the cottage where we had seen the unpleasant Sicilian countryman; he was, we noticed, peering at us from his half open door, and it was clear that we did not have to look farther for the source of our betrayal. We were not too bewildered to call out uncomplimentary remarks, and to make meaningful gestures, miming the ear to ear slitting of the throat. These gestures and the accompanying abuse were ignored by our captors. We were escorted to the road where, parked by the verge, was a light German truck marked with the insignia of the Afrika Korps. We were thrust unceremoniously into the back and driven to the neighbouring town of Ragusa. The truck pulled up in front of a fair-sized white building that looked as if it could have been the Town Hall. It was not, however, the mayor who greeted us.

We were thrust at bayonet-point into a room on the second floor and lined up in front of a large table littered with papers, telephones, typewriters and other official impedimenta. Behind the table, wearing civilian clothes, peering at us through rimless glasses, sat the flesh and blood embodiment of the villainous Gestapo chief that I had seen in a score of films. With pasty face and soulless blue eyes he was as about alluring as a bird-eating spider. As soon as he saw us there before him, bearded, filthy and rheumy-eyed with weariness, he started barking questions in the approved Hollywood manner. Suddenly his tirade, which had sounded like a succession of bursts from a bad-tempered machine-gun, ceased in mid-volley, and I saw our inquisitor's cobra eyes fixed on me – where a slight but obvious bulge appeared in my ancient jacket just above the waistline. He threw back his chair and, moving with surprising speed, hurled himself round the table and grabbed me. One podgy white hand dived inside my jacket, in search, no doubt, of the pocket radio he suspected to be concealed in my bosom. There was a slight upheaval, followed by a yelp of pain. He recoiled and withdrew his hand, which was dripping with good Aryan blood.

Cressida had struck her blow for freedom. Now surely Nemesis would strike me down.

Feeling, if I felt anything, that I had really no more to lose, except life itself, I put my hand into my jacket; Cressida scrambled aboard and I withdrew her into the daylight. There we stood, Cressida and I, exposed to the full fury of this powerful representative of the Third Reich. I glanced at Cressida, her hackles raised, her wings hanging as she mantled, her eyes glowing like red coals.

The expected revolver shot never came. I looked at the Gestapo officer, who had retreated a few steps; his pallid face was, if anything, whiter than ever. I glanced at the armed escort, the henchmen behind the table; all were speechless, but when I looked longer I saw they were inarticulate with ill-supressed laughter! At last the commander of our escort said something which I interpreted as an invitation to tell our story, which I did at length. The question as to how we escaped or what we planned to do never arose. By now the Gestapo chief had to some extent recovered his self-control. He had, for the moment at least, been knocked off his pedestal, but it took a British kestrel to do it.

Soon the Germans were in full cry again; *Raus! Raus!* but after the terror of the last few moments their voices sounded like music to my ears. I put Cressida, calmer now, her dignity restored, back into my jacket; we were herded into the street and from thence into the waiting truck. We noticed that the attitude of the Germans had perceptibly changed; they even shared their cigarettes and water bottles with us as we wound our long and circuitous way back into the hills, and back to captivity.

Our reception by the Italian staff at Campo P.G. 98 was frigid, but the German commandant must have said something in our favour, because none of the expected penalties followed and, instead of being sent to the Callaboose for days of solitary confinement, we were returned to the main camp. The only precautions taken were that the five of us were split up, each being sent to a different compound, just in case we should be tempted to repeat the performance. I never saw the others again and I can only hope they all survived the next two years. They were certainly four of the best comrades a man could have had.

Now life went on much as if the escape had never happened. My interest turned again to natural history. The Black-veined Whites and Bath White butterflies had given place to Red Admirals, Painted Ladies, and a host of spectacular Fritillaries. Hawk moths of all sorts blundered into our tents at night and once I caught, and examined before releasing, a magnificent specimen of the Spurge Hawk moth, an insect of extreme rarity in Britain. Cressida still accompanied me for walks about the hilly rock-strewn compound, and caught enough mice and wall lizards to keep her in perfect health and plumage.

Morale amongst the P.O.W.s was high. German resistance had collapsed in North Africa and the invasion of Sicily was just a matter of time; soon we would all be free once more. The Italian guards were quite frank in their belief that the hated Germans, the *Tedesci*, would evacuate the island without a shot being fired. We had our doubts about this. We heard that the camp was to be evacuated and that we were going to the Italian mainland.

All sorts of escape plans were considered and cast aside as impractical. I half thought of hiding in the camp until it was evacuated and then once more taking to the mountains, but this time I had been unable to accumulate enough rations and I suspected also that the camp commandant and his assistants were keeping a wary, if unobtrusive, eye on my movements. I had thought it possible that I could contact a friendly local family, who might be able to hide and feed me until the end of hostilities, or at least until Italy had been invaded and I had a chance to get back to the Allied lines. Against this was the knowledge of the terrible revenge wreaked by the Germans on any civilians even faintly suspected of helping the Allied cause, and I decided I did not want that on my conscience. In addition to all this it was widely rumoured that the Italian government were on the point of concluding a separate peace which, we were assured, would mean that we would all be immediately freed.

Be that as it may, one morning in June found us, with such of our personal possessions as we could carry, meandering in untidy and broken array to the local station, where a train awaited to take us to our new camp. I sat back in a corner of the carriage and relaxed. Cressida sat on my knee, looking out of the window as the train began its long, slow, serpentine climb between the mountains; their snow-capped peaks shone with a pinkish glow in the sunlight as we rattled and jerked our way towards Messina at the extreme northern tip of Sicily. I quite enjoyed the journey; at least I didn't have to make any decisions. I could doze and dream, and on waking gaze at some of Europe's loveliest and most dramatic scenery.

We arrived at Messina eventually and there, waiting for us, was a tiny steamer which must have been used in happier times as the ferry between Sicily and Reggio on the extreme southern tip of Italy's toe. Everyone, P.O.W.s, guards and ship's crew, seemed in a holiday mood; after all, why shouldn't they be? The war was virtually over, or so they had all decided; and, such is the Italian philosophy, it would quickly be forgotten. The little ship was soon on its way and Cressida seemed to enjoy the short crossing; at least she was soon sunbathing happily as she perched on a life-belt which was conveniently fixed in a sheltered position on the deck. The sea voyage was over far too quickly and once more we were in a train, slogging up from Reggio towards Naples. We arrived at Naples well after dark and in the middle of an air-raid. We were to get more than our share of these in the weeks ahead.

The new camp, P.G. 66, at Capua, a few miles from Naples, was a very different affair from the one we had left behind. For one thing it had been established since the early days of the fighting in North Africa; in it were prisoners taken in Tobruk, Benghazi and the Libyan desert campaigns. It was well organised; there were a reasonable number of regular Red Cross parcels and the accommodation was in huts, instead of tents as before. There was even an extremely proficient dance band, that gave alfresco concerts several times a week. But above all the camp was famous as the scene of a fantastic escape that had taken place before our arrival. Apparently some-one had discovered a man-hole inside the camp perimeter and, during a severe thunderstorm, practically the entire population of P.O.W.s had literally queued up, together with their Red Cross parcels and personal possessions, had descended this rather unromantic road to freedom and emerged later from the sewers in part of the city of Naples. Although, I believe, no one actually got home, it was such a splendid effort and so original that a special song was composed and was always known as the camp signature tune.

Here for the first time since being captured I found that I had enough food, even a little to spare. We developed the custom of inviting each other to tea or supper parties, where we ate cakes made of klim powder, sultanas, milk, squashed biscuits and cheese, which may sound nauseating but which did, in fact, taste uncommonly good. Here again, as in all Italian camps, mice and lizards abounded and Cressida did well enough. Here, too, she lived in perfect freedom and as before showed no particular wish to venture beyond the enclosing wire.

One addition to the fauna worth mentioning were the toads. Each evening at dusk, as the perimeter lights went on, numbers of huge toads, just like their British relations but somewhat larger, appeared as if by magic, hopping and crawling about the huts and alleyways. Nobody interfered with them, and no doubt they did their bit to keep down the fleas, lice and any other, all too prevalent, vermin. Cressida must have realised that these attractive amphibians were almost inedible, as she made no attempt to molest them, other than a half-hearted effort to chase them about the floor. She occasionally pounced on one tiny victim but released it at once unharmed.

Our days were enlivened by regular visits from the American Air Force, who came over so high that their great Flying Fortresses looked like tiny, silvery fish swimming in the sapphire-blue bowl of the sky: soon came the whistle of falling bombs followed by the muffled crump and blast that seemed to make the whole earth shake. We knew that the target was the town of Naples and its environs, but we were none too happy about it, as there were no shelters in the camp. We could do nothing save crowd to the doors of our huts and hope for the best, whilst very much fearing, if not actually expecting, the worst. The anticipated invasion of Sicily had come and the Allies, as we had expected, were meeting stiff opposition in an almost impossibly difficult country to invade; it looked as if it would be a long and uphill grind, which indeed it was.

Now, once more, we were to move as an assault on the Italian peninsula was expected. This time it was farther north to a camp in Bologna, where, in September 1943, we heard of the Italian capitulation. The guards went wild with excitement and soon were more or less incapable with *vino*. This was, of course, the time to break out and take to the countryside. But somehow a rumour started, which was accepted by the higher ranks amongst the British P.O.W.s, that all prisoners were to remain inside their camps to await the arrival of the Allies. In fact, we were told that anyone who used his initiative would, on his eventual return to Britain, be court-martialled for disobeying orders. Later I heard that several inmates of other camps defied this order and managed to get through to their own lines and to a hero's welcome. I know that I, and a number of my friends at Bologna, felt thoroughly frustrated about the whole business.

The next morning, sure enough, up rolled the Germans, supported by artillery. It was then by no means certain whether the Germans intended to evacuate us, or to blow us to Kingdom come. We were not kept long in doubt; the gates swung open and in they poured, clattering and rattling their arms, singing their same old song, *Raus! Raus! Raus!* The only consolation, though a poor one, was that the Italian guards, our one-time custodians, had all been disarmed and were being loaded into trucks as ignominiously captive as the rest of us. Thus did the Tiger treat the Jackal.

The same old weary routine was to follow. The same hot, dusty and sticky march to yet another equally hot, sticky and dusty cattle-truck waiting, as usual, in the same sort of siding, and with the usual almost oven-like temperature within. As we marched through the streets trying to put up some sort of show of pride and self-respect it seemed that almost the entire civilian population of Bologna were lining the streets, but this time we were the Allies and the Germans the hated foes. Some of the women, far braver than their men folk, shrieked obscenities at our impassive escort, who chose to ignore these insults. The crowds not only shouted messages of good cheer to us, but were also bent on teasing and harassing the Germans as much as possible.

Suddenly, a prisoner, marching two files ahead of me, and on the right-hand outside column, did a sort of half-rolling somersault and plunged into the crowd, who divided, re-formed, and swallowed him instantly. It was one of the neatest tricks that I have ever seen. The much plagued guards either failed to spot this manœuvre or else were too preoccupied in shepherding the rest of us to take any decisive action.

Our accommodation, we found on arrival, was to be much the same as on our journey up from Algiers to Tunisia, except that now the windows of the cattle-truck, such as they were, had been tightly barred and cross-barred with vicious-looking barbed wire. Furthermore, each truckload of allied P.O.W.s was accompanied by four armed guards in field-grey uniforms. The Italians, on the other hand, were less closely guarded because the Germans presumably did not credit them with the initiative to escape. In this, at least, they misjudged their former accomplices because we know that one truckload, if not more, succeeded in filing through or unravelling the wire, and at some wayside halt the whole lot nipped out of the window and swiftly disappeared into the protective shelter of the omnipresent vineyards.

Personally I felt too dispirited to do more than hope that sooner or later a fresh opportunity would arise. That night we must have crossed the famous Brenner Pass because early next morning we pulled into the station at Spittal, high in the Austrian Tyrol. Here again was a setting of supreme loveliness; high above the town soared the great craggy, thrilling shapes of the Alps. I have always loved mountains and to me the Tyrolean Alps are mountains without peer. I thought, as I trudged towards yet another prison camp, of chamois, alpine choughs and golden eagles. I did not have far to look for alpine choughs — every rooftop was lined with these inky jack-daw-sized birds, with their brilliant red legs, curved yellow bills, and their high-pitched querulous call-notes.

The Stalag in which Cressida and I now found ourselves was a transit camp, wherein were assembled representatives of all the armed forces who had fought in Northern Africa; it was a melting pot and junction to which all those who had been caught unprepared by the Italian Armistice were sent for documentation and eventual transfer to other permanent camps in the heart of the Fatherland. One of the first people I met on arrival was John Oldfield, whom I had last seen at the Green Howards' depot in 1939. He had been, until his capture, adjutant of a battalion of that regiment, and had been put in the bag in the Western Desert. I introduced him to Cressida and told him our history to date. He was, I think, slightly perturbed to see that I was now of such humble rank. None the less he arranged for me to move into his quarters and he introduced me to his friends, whose vicissitudes he had been sharing for some time. He must have been in a position of some authority in the camp because I remember he immediately sent for the British cook sergeant, who was responsible for dishing up the meals for the officers, and asked him to produce some raw meat for Cressida, which was done with remarkable speed.

The next day I was approached by two captains of the South African Army, who were planning an escape. Exactly what these plans involved I do not know; all I do know is that it necessitated them moving from the officers' quarters to those of the other ranks. It was also imperative that two erstwhile privates should replace them in the officers' quarters. I was asked if I was prepared to help them out and of course agreed. The immediate result of this was that I, together with another private soldier, one John Williams, a schoolmaster in peace-time, were interviewed by the senior British officer of the camp and promoted to lieutenant on the spot. This must have been one of the speediest and most unorthodox promotions in British military history.

Now I was back where I started, with two pips on my shoulder once again. I moved into the officers' mess which was, in fact, not much less uncomfortable than those I had previously occupied. The only major difference was that now, as an officer, I did not have to do any work and was entitled to a certain grudging respect. I even, on occasion, received a salute from the lower orders of the German Army. It was a somewhat musical comedy situation, but at least it was not of my choosing. So Cressida and I lived once more with the élite, and we would have to watch our steps in the new and honourable situation in which we now found ourselves. The two officers made their escape and were never heard of again in Germany; they were believed to have made their way to freedom.

Hardly had Cressida and I adjusted ourselves to our new role than we were on the move again, this time to Stalag 18B at Muhlberg-on-Elbe in north Germany. After much the same sort of journey as all the others we had experienced we arrived at Muhlberg, which was situated in one of the least attractive parts of Germany; the country was flat and desolate, with field after field of sugar-beet and other root vegetables. This camp, like the last, was divided into two sections, officers and other ranks. It was under the command of a *Wachtmeister*, a rank which, I gather, is equivalent to that of a sort of regimental-sergeant-major of cavalry. This chap was an ex-priest or had been studying for Holy Orders before the war; he was a pleasant enough personality and did what he could to make us more comfortable. What was most disconcerting to me was that he insisted on taking charge of Cressida during our stay. Cressida and I had never been separated since our first meeting on Romney Marsh nearly a year previously, and I did not think much of the idea. She was, however, given pretty good accommodation in a light and airy shed. The *Wachtmeister* himself provided her with meat from his own rather meagre ration, and I visited her once a day under armed guard, to assure her that this was a strictly temporary arrangement.

As it turned out it was probably all for the best, because our own meat rations were virtually non-existent and we lived on potatoes and black bread – and very little of either. The only fat we were given was a colourless, tasteless form of margarine, which was popularly believed to be axle-grease. This I can well believe. Each week we were given a piece of so-called cheese, and this according to rumour was made from some side product of coal dust. I can believe this too. There was also a weekly ration of *Sauerkraut*. This had a singularly unpleasant, but somehow familiar, odour, and after the first week we refused it to a man. We had discovered that the factory where it was made was staffed by British other ranks and European slave labour who, we were assured, to do their best for the Cause and to help bring Germany to her knees, used to urinate on it at every opportunity.

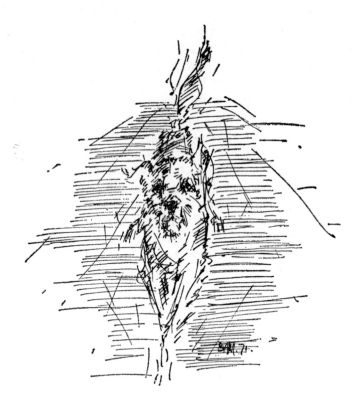

Chapter 16

I⊤ must have been about this time that I met Frank
Elton. Frank, a South African, who had been in civilian
life registrar to a well-known judge and had intended to
make law his profession, already had several escapes to
his credit. At the time of our meeting he had just joined
the camp, having been recaptured after jumping off a
train near the Brenner Pass; he had been at large for
some weeks and had nearly succeeded in crossing the
Swiss Frontier. I shall always remember the first time I
saw him. He had just come out of a period of solitary
confinement following this escape. That morning we were

to be moved to what was supposed to be our final and permanent camp on the Czech border. I had just retrieved Cressida from the Wachtmeister's custody and was busy getting my few possessions together prior to the move. Frank was lying at full length in his bunk, quietly drinking a cup of coffee. He began asking about Cressida, inquiring if she was a jackdaw, an insult I found it hard to forgive.

The Germans were '*rausing*' like madmen, but Frank ignored them completely, even when they started using their bayonets in a way that I thought decidedly unfriendly. 'You must remember Sir Francis Drake, old boy,' he said to me. 'He finished his game of bowls and I am going to finish my bloody coffee, so sit down and don't flap; it's going to be a long war.' Frank was an impressive figure, well over six feet tall, with shoulders like a front row forward, which indeed he had been, and the biggest, blackest, bushiest beard I had ever seen. He would have been at home on the deck of a privateer with a patch over one eye, and the Jolly Roger flying above him. He spoke both German and Russian as well as Afrikaans, and he had an incurable weakness for needling the Germans at every opportunity.

On this occasion the prisoners outside were lined up and waiting to march off. Frank was still languishing in his bunk, savouring the last drop of coffee. Two guards entered shouting at us and began probing with their bayonets the corners of the hut and any place likely to conceal a possible escaper. Frank watched them idly then, with a sardonic grin, asked in German, 'What are you searching for? Are you looking for Adolf?' The guards did not find this amusing.

From the time of our meeting Frank and I were inseparable. Having finished his coffee and admonished me for swallowing mine in too great haste, Frank collected his belongings, which were contained in an enormous, bulging, mountaineer's rucksack, and we joined the others outside. Frank had **already decided** to escape on this journey, naturally assuming that I would go with him. He assured me he had enough food in his pack to last us a week, so we would not have to worry about that. We chose two seats near the window and sat and relaxed in comfort to await our chance, which we knew was many hours' distant. Ours was an ordinary passenger train and, apart from the two guards who sat by the door, could have been any tourist train carrying holidaymakers on a tour of the Fatherland.

The train wound its way across the flat farmland of northern Germany. Each field seemed to contain one or more hares which appeared to be much darker and heftier than ours at home. I thought with nostalgia of Bracken, and in my mind's eye I could picture her, ears and tail streaming in the wind, as her quarry was sighted. The flat pastures were ideal for a 'long-dog' to show its paces. Cressida, re-united with me, seemed to enjoy the soothing motion of the train and looked out of the window, apparently as intent on the passing scenery as I was. The guards were quite relaxed and were soon joking and laughing at Frank's quips. I knew that they had been lulled into a sense of false security, which we did our utmost to encourage. We made an excuse to visit the lavatory and we noted the general layout. A group of guards were gathered at one end of the corridor playing cards. The windows were unprotected and were of the type, common to British trains, that slid up and down, controlled by a leather strap.

By late afternoon the low-lying agricultural land had been replaced by scattered woodlands, which rapidly gave place to forests. Then the train began to climb into the hills. We were approaching the Czech Frontier. Here the desolate look of the passing countryside was increased by new fallen snow. Black pine forests stood stark and grim against the icy landscape. Peering from the warmth of the carriage I saw in a forest clearing, sharply silhouetted against the snowy background, the gaunt and sinister figure of a solitary wolf. At that moment I was vividly reminded of a picture which made a great impression on me as a child. It hung in my grandmother's drawing-room and depicted a wolf crossing a frozen stream, across which lay a snow-covered branch. The wolf's eyes shone in the gathering dusk and his nose was lowered as he quested the traces of some fugitive quarry. The picture was called '*Einsam*,' 'A Lonely One.' I used to stand beneath this picture and ponder deeply. Here, at last, was this self-same wolf come thrillingly to life. The very background, save only for the stream, was the same; warm and comfortable as I was I could somehow feel the creeping evening chill, the loneliness and the tameless savagery of that solitary wolf, seen so fleetingly from the train window.

Darkness was now closing down in earnest. We ate some of our rations of *Bludwurst*, and sour-tasting black bread, and as the train plunged into the Czechoslovakian borderland, we waited ready to seize our opportunity if and when it arose. The guards were both asleep; noticing this, the prisoner sitting nearest to them stuffed a motley collection of cigarette ends, dead matches and bits of paper into the barrels of their rifles. He must have been remarkably adroit because neither of the guards raised their lolling heads. It never occurred to any of us that, should they fire their rifles in the confined space of the carriage, any unfortunate P.O.W. who happened to be nearby would probably be blown to smithereens if the barrels burst as we intended. We had not confided in our carriage mates, but they must have guessed that something was afoot.

Frank and I did a reconnaissance, stepping over the feet of the slumbering guards and sliding back the door as silently as possible; to our amazement the guards slept on. The four guards at the far end of the corridor were still engrossed in their game of cards; apart from a casual glance as I opened the lavatory door they took little notice of us. We stood for some time by the window of the corridor, apparently lost in thought, and they did not once look up. Our plan was simple enough. We intended to wait until the train next reached an incline and, as soon as it had slowed down sufficiently, we would leave the train via the window and jump for it. We would then cross into Czechoslovakia and try to contact members of the local resistance movement.

The time was approaching for action. We sat opposite each other and tried to relax; we smoked, for lack of anything better, some particularly nauseous French cigarettes called, most inappropriately, *Élégantes*. I tucked Cressida into my jacket, who had now become quite resigned to this sort of thing. On the spur of the moment we decided to enlist the help of two fellow officers. Their role was to be entirely passive. They were to stand nonchalantly, looking out of the window, between us and the guards at the end of the corridor. The signal was to be a muffled cough.

The train had started its climb; grunting and straining it was moving at little more than walking pace. We gave the signal, and our two accomplices rose. We had not closed home the compartment door after our recce, and it slid open without a sound. The two guards still slept on unawares. One of the officers was signalling frantically. We moved quickly; the train was slowly gathering speed again. Out in the corridor we found that the guards had gone. We gently closed the door and opened the carriage window, the rush of snow-laden air nearly choking us. Frank grabbed the top of the window, put his legs out, wriggled sideways and was gone — gone, that is, except for his enormous pack; we had never measured it, and this was a problem we should have, but had not, foreseen.

Now there was Frank dangling in mid-air, with the train rapidly accelerating. I prayed the straps would hold; I struggled and pushed but, strain as I might, I could not push it out. It was a grim experience. I expected at any minute to see Frank flattened against the face of the mountain as we entered a tunnel. Frank, of course, realised the position and was now struggling desperately to get back through the window. I grabbed the pack and pulled with all my might. Frank must have weighed all of fifteen stone, and how the straps held his weight heaven alone knows. One of the other officers came to our aid and at last Frank managed to get one arm back in; I then somehow managed to get my arms round his chest, pulled hard, and we landed in a heap on the corridor floor. The escape was over before it began, but at least Frank was alive.

Fortune must have been with us that night. Not only had Frank survived an exceedingly tricky situation and emerged undaunted in body and spirit but, on our somewhat crestfallen return to the carriage, we found our escorts still slumbering on untroubled. They were, in fact, a pair of elderly Bavarian countrymen who had been conscripted; had we escaped they would no doubt have been court-martialled for negligence and probably suffered the severest of penalties. The main fear of these fellows was that they would be sent to the Russian Front, a fate which awaited those who transgressed even in the smallest degree.

Despite the struggle in which I had so unexpectedly taken part, Cressida, who had been inside my jacket throughout, was quite unruffled; she had somehow managed to work her way round to the small of my back, where she was out of the way of the turmoil.

Now, our effort having been in vain, we relaxed again and spent the rest of the night chatting, dozing and smoking our unspeakable French cigarettes. Sometime during the next morning we arrived at Marish Trubaw, a tiny scattered village lying in the foothills of the Sudeten mountains, well inside the Czechoslovakian border.

Camp Oflag IVB was a splendid affair, entirely different

from anything I had experienced before. Built, I believe, originally as a luxury hotel, it had been commandeered, first as a training establishment for officers and finally as a prison camp. There were, on average, about eight of us to a room. The grounds were wooded and extensive and there was even a splendid outdoor swimming-bath which we made good use of during the spring. Here, within the encircling wire, the camp was run more or less on the lines of an infantry battalion, being divided into companies.

Apart from the fact that we were behind wire, and under the ultimate control of the German prison staff, the place just about ran itself. Each morning and evening there was a roll-call or *Apel*, for which we were mustered into groups of five; after a good deal of deliberate obstruction, designed to annoy the German authorities, we were counted and then dismissed. For the rest of the time we were free (if that is the right word) to follow such occupations as we could. There was a very good library, and there were lectures; I gave one on falconry with Cressida as my model. There was also the Green Room Club, a group of amateur actors.

The Indian Army officers, of which there were quite a large number, including Sikhs, Marathas and Gurkhas, put on their own shows. These were excellent, but unfortunately the dialogue was unintelligible to most of us. One play included a scene in which the maharajah, hawk on fist, was supposed to appear on stage surrounded by his guard of honour, courtiers and sari-clad lovelies. Unfortunately Cressida, who was masquerading as the maharajah's noble hunting falcon, saw the light on the stage while waiting for her cue in the wings. She flew out, did a circuit of the stage, and was then swallowed up in the enveloping darkness of the auditorium, where she remained for the rest of the performance. She took part in several productions and normally acquitted herself well enough, but she was, I suppose, entitled to a certain amount of artistic temperament.

We did not get any chances to escape here, because all the would-be escapers had to submit their plans to an Escape Committee, known for security reasons as The Toasting Committee, and there was a waiting list as long as my arm. I cannot recall any successful escapes, although a number of highly original plans were conceived. There was, of course, a radio in the camp and, try as they would, the Germans never found it. We used to get the B.B.C. news every night and so were kept up to date with the progress of the war. The Germans, every now and then, would make unexpected searches of the block where they imagined it to be concealed; to counteract these the 'Cloak and Dagger Boys' would post look-outs at strategic positions. At the sight of any grey-clad figure appearing they would yell out 'Goon up,' and the cry would be taken up by man after man as the set was spirited away.

We arrived at Marish Trubaw in early November, and remained until the late spring of 1944. Luckily there was a good supply of Red Cross parcels and so, with the combined ingenuity of the British cooks and the catering officer, we managed to feed reasonably well. In addition, my mother used to send me personal parcels from home; these contained such items as socks, gloves, underclothes and, above all, chocolate and cigarettes. I did not smoke much in those days, but English cigarettes were an in-fallible means of barter. The German sentries would do virtually anything for Players or Kensitas, and I used to exchange some of mine for large quantities of horse flesh, which not only helped to keep Cressida in splendid fettle, but which Frank and I used to cook for ourselves during our periodical brew-ups. These took place in the cellars, our air-raid shelters, beneath the actual building. These brew-ups were a much-treasured routine amongst the prisoners; on entering these vaults one would encounter dozens of satanic figures, faces aglow in the light of their own particular fires.

Frank and I had long had a mutual pact. It had been

agreed that anything we received in our personal parcels we would share 50–50; thus if I received two pairs of socks, Frank would have one pair; bars of chocolate were divided and so were tins of cigarettes. As it happened, I received a number of parcels which were so divided, and this went on for weeks, Frank getting more and more embarrassed as his parcels failed to materialise. It did not worry me as Frank was a great friend, who helped me in many ways. He was particularly adept at cajoling and bullying the Germans into parting with such items as electric light bulbs, fresh eggs and cheese; so it was on the whole a very well-balanced partnership. But my parcels still kept coming and Frank had not received a single one. Then at last, great news. The postal officer sent for Frank; a parcel had arrived at last from Johannesburg. Together we charged off to the camp post office, where a parcel of generous proportions was waiting. Frank signed for it and off we loped to our room with visions of a gargantuan feast before us. We fumbled with what seemed to be endless yards of string and acres of crisp brown wrapping paper. At last we got it open. Frank seized the final corner of paper and tore it off expecting to reveal the long-expected medley of chocolate, jam, biscuits and fruit. Instead there lay exposed to our horrified gaze eight brand new volumes of South African Constitutional Law. Without a word, Frank handed me four of them; he had kept his part of the bargain.

Frank's father had not, as one might have supposed, an exceptionally perverse sense of humour. According to the letter enclosed he honestly believed that the German authorities, together with the Red Cross, provided all that was needed to support our bodies, and the only additional nourishment required was for the mind. He had a lot of explaining to do later.

Spring came at last to Marish Trubaw and with it came flocks of Serins, the little yellowish green finches that are, in fact, close relations to domestic canaries. Redstarts and the rarer Black redstarts, with their charcoal bodies and flaming tails, would hop around our feet, hoping for trifles of biscuits or cheese. The wooded slopes echoed with the mewing of courting buzzards, who hung suspended in the sky over their chosen nesting sites, or passed high overhead on their great rounded moth-like wings.

Cressida enjoyed the strengthening sun and would spend hours sitting on low branches in many parts of the camp or else indulging in her favourite pursuit, a long and thorough dust bath in the rich loamy soil beneath her favourite pine tree.

Early one morning I was walking round the perimeter of the camp when I heard the chinking of a scared black-bird. I looked up casually and instantly froze; only a few yards away, so close that every detail stood out, was a magnificent female goshawk. She was exactly like the one depicted on the screen in my aunt's bedroom, which had so fascinated me as a child. The blackbird had taken refuge in the centre of the wire barricade, which had been constructed to keep us within bounds, and was resolutely refusing to leave. The goshawk, her crest slightly raised, was in full yarak and meant to have her quarry. She was clutching the wire with both feet and making threatening darting movements at the blackbird which, however, seemed as secure amongst the strands of wire as he would have been deep inside a holly bush. I must have made some slight sound, as she turned her head; for a second her marigold eyes blazed into mine, then she was gone. She left a memory I shall treasure always.

As the spring drew on, so did the Russian offensive intensify; the talk was all of the expected second Front, which we believed would soon be launched. The Germans were falling back in the east, we learned of various commando raids on the coast of France, and nightly we heard the distant drone of aircraft on their way to and from Berlin. Now we knew that the end was in sight. We used to speculate on the outcome and how it would affect us. The logical conclusion was that, after the Western Allies had consolidated their position, the Germans would sue for peace. We would be released and all go home happily to a well-merited welcome. There were those amongst us, however, who were convinced that we would either all be shot out of hand as a last defiant gesture or that we would be transported *en masse* to some obscure fortress in the Bavarian Alps, where we would be held as pawns in a sinister game of international intrigue. Neither of these suppositions did much to ease the unspoken, but ever present, atmosphere of foreboding that we all must have suffered to some degree.

The Germans had their own ideas, and thus in May 1944 we found ourselves once more on a train, this time heading westward towards Brunswick. This was a journey with a difference. It appeared that some time previously the British Commandos on one of their probing raids had captured a number of the enemy. According to the Germans these had been handcuffed on their return to Britain as prisoners. How much truth there was in this story I do not know, but I do know that we ourselves were now handcuffed and an odd experience it was. Though ignominious, however, it was not quite such a gruesome ordeal as one might imagine. The handcuffs were connected by chains long enough to allow reasonable comfort; moreover, it did not take us long to discover that they could be opened by the manipulation of an ordinary key from a sardine tin. Thus we soon had them off, only to replace them on arrival.

Our new camp was formerly a Luftwaffe Cadet Training Establishment. It was in a landscape very like the Surrey countryside, all pine trees, heaths, gorse bushes and broom thickets. This was ideal country for hobbies, but I was never lucky enough to see any there. Our accommodation, too, was the sort to be found anywhere in the military zone of Aldershot or Farnborough. The main difference was its situation; close to a Messerschmitt factory on one side and an alleged V1 launching site on the other, with the main Brunswick autobahn just out of sight to the south. One can only assume that our hosts, with a somewhat perverted sense of humour, had placed us there strategically in the hope that when these targets were destroyed by the R.A.F. or U.S.A.F. we would all go up with them, a cheerful thought. Alternatively they might have believed that, with a large prison camp in the vicinity, the Allies would avoid the area. In that case they were wrong indeed, and we lived under the perpetual threat of annihilation by day and night.

There were air-raid shelters of a sort beneath each block, but it is highly improbable that they would have been much use against a direct hit. Regularly the air-raid sirens would sound and as regularly, after an interval of a few minutes, feeling utterly helpless, we would hear the barking of the local Ack-Ack guns. Soon the sky towards the west would flicker and glint as the sun caught the approaching Armada. At night the Lancasters took over and the heavens reverberated to the roar of their engines, to be followed all too soon by a sound rather like thick carpets being beaten with heavy sticks a long way away; and the ground would rise and fall as the blast followed on the heels of the exploding block-busters. Every night would find us down below in the cellars, and here the Green Room Club really came into its own. They used to put on revues and cabaret-type entertainment with a strictly topical bias that was quite excellent; and above all they served their purpose, which was to make us forget what was going on around us.

However, it was only a matter of time before the camp was blasted. On one fine morning Frank and I were talking to a group of Gurkha officers. Cressida was sitting at the top of a stunted pine right in the centre of the compound. This was one of her favourite observation posts, where she could keep an eye on what was going on beneath, and in particular the movement of some incautious vole or field-mouse. It was, in fact, known as Cressida's Tree. The air-raid sirens went as usual, and the bombers were overhead, but to-day they did not continue on their way but started circling ominously. Frank and I looked at each other; 'This is it,' we thought.

There was a slit trench nearby and the Gurkhas had already dived into it, shouting to us to join them. I looked at Cressida perched fifteen to twenty feet above my head, showed my fist and called her; but she ignored me completely. In desperation I shinned up the tree, which luckily had some projections, grabbed her unceremoniously, getting well clawed in the process, slid down and dived into the trench. As I hit the ground there was a whining roar and a shattering, shuddering crash worthy of Judgment Day. Earth and stones came pouring over us, and this was followed by a number of similar but smaller explosions — anti-personnel mines. For moments we lay there half buried, expecting extinction at any moment; sticks of bombs fell round the perimeter, then at last the droning died away in the distance. We raised our heads and looked about us. Where Cressida's tree had stood there now yawned a sizeable crater; of the tree itself only a blackened splinter remained. This raid cost the lives of a number of officers who had been caught in the open; the camp was never actually bombed again, although we had one or two close shaves.

The news of D-Day and the fall of Rome, both received within a few days of each other, put new heart into every one of us. But still the months dragged on; there was the gallant failure at Arnhem, which affected us only inasmuch as prisoners captured there arrived in the camp and were able to keep us up-to-date with what was going on outside and, more important to us, as to the possible duration of the war. The autumn passed and winter drew on; Christmas came and with it the last desperate counterattack in the Ardennes, which we feared might prolong hostilities by months; however, it was quickly checked and the Allies drove on slowly but remorselessly.

Christmas 1944 was a cheerful, if not over-festive, affair; we had enough Red Cross parcels to provide some sort of substitute for the real thing. We had our home-brewed raisin wine; this was excellent stuff, highly alcoholic, made of raisins, yeast and sugar. It was brewed in the china electric-light shades, flattish bowls with high rims, and fermented by time and the steady warmth of the light bulbs. We all knew by then that our release could only be a matter of a few months at the worst. I was cheered by a letter from home in which my mother sent special messages for Cressida, the indomitable. This helped to make Christmas, even in the bag, the sort of day it was intended to be.

Spring came round again, my third since leaving England. I used to wake at dawn, shivering under my one threadbare blanket, my back bruised through contact with the too few, too hard, bedboards, most of which had been sacrificed in the interests of cooking or in keeping our solitary half-hearted stove alive. As I lay there I listened to the songs of the local blackbirds and thrushes, and I compared their performance with those I had known in Sussex and to which I would, if my luck held out, soon be returning. In just the same way I had lain sleepless as a small boy at my prep school in the last week of the Easter Term. I would listen to the blackbirds fluting and the cheerful oft-repeated notes of the song thrushes and mistle thrushes. These German birds sang well, very well, but somehow they just weren't the same as our blackbirds and thrushes at home.

Cressida, who by now must have been at least four years old, was deep in moult again, dropping her hand-some chestnut-and-black primaries and tail feathers everywhere. When she roused, shaking herself like a dog, a cloud of the tiny, fluffy body feathers would fly out and sink gently to the floor. She had, during the last winter, proved herself to be incredibly adaptable in the matter of diet; with virtually no training she had learned to eat bully beef and even tinned salmon, and for a period of some weeks, when horseflesh was virtually unobtainable, she had existed almost exclusively on these unusual viands. When, after a week or two, I gave her a large, fat and luscious mouse, she ate it without any great show of excitement, and the following morning produced an oval and apparently perfectly healthy cast. This was completely at variance with the books, which state emphatically that, unless given a quota of fur or feather at least twice a week, a hawk is certain to die. It would appear that Cressida had not read books of this nature, because she throve mightily and was now replacing her feathers with new ones of equal vigour to the last.

Then one morning she vanished; she had been sitting on the window-sill of our room, glorying in the early morning sunlight. When I went to collect her for a period of flying exercise she just wasn't there, and no one had seen her leave. I asked everyone if they had seen her; I organised a massed search; I even recruited a hunting-party amongst the German guards, who by now knew her well. Every tree and bush in the camp was examined and re-examined. I even penetrated into the darkness of the air-raid shelter; there was nothing, not even a fallen feather, to hint as to her whereabouts. We had been inseparable, sharing everything for more than two years; to lose her now was unthinkable.

All that day I hunted and called her; all the following night I lay sleepless, sick with despair. It seemed as if more than half my own personality had seeped away. Had she been an ordinary kestrel, under ordinary circumstances, I would have accepted the situation though, no doubt, have felt sad and disappointed. But now I realised more than ever before how much she meant to me; she had boosted me up in times of worry, fear and despair; she had given me a reason for living and a determination to win through; she had been my lode star, and now she had gone. Frank understood and did his best to cheer me up. I must have seemed a poor fish to the others, although they never showed it. Feeling half drugged with weariness and misery I stumbled round the camp grounds at dawn; Frank and a few other volunteers split up and quartered the whole area. Then, carried faintly on the breeze, I thought I heard a familiar sound. Desperately I ran in the direction from which I thought it had come. Nothing, nothing whatsoever. Then again came the familiar keek-keeking. I looked with eager eyes, and saw her, a tiny dark figure perched on the chimney of the guard-room, well beyond the boundary wire. I called her with as much authority as I could, and at once she came; skimming in fast and high she put in a half-stoop, checked, and planed down to land on my upheld fist. Where she had been for the last twenty-four hours was immaterial; Cressida was back. The very progress of the war lost its significance for a moment. The rest of the search-party arrived, and they seemed almost as pleased as I was at the truant's return. Cressida was not unduly hungry, but condescended to eat a piece of horseflesh especially procured to emulate the fatted calf.

A few weeks later German resistance in the west virtually collapsed; daily the guns of the American Ninth Army could be heard as they pounded their way nearer. Typhoons and Mustangs hedge-hopped over the camp on their missions of destruction. One morning at dawn we were aroused by the sound of shells whizzing over our heads; a battle was in progress virtually outside the camp gates. As the light increased so the firing grew heavier, until it seemed that a shot was likely to remove the roof of the building in which we lay. The S.B.O. called a conference, and told us to remain below and to await events. We hadn't long to wait; the firing slackened and ceased and all was quiet, a hush laden with expectancy. Soon a heavy rumbling could be heard behind the surrounding pines and we rushed to the gates; tanks, jeeps and armoured cars came rocking and swaying around the corner and up the road to the main gates which were now flung open. The Americans had arrived and we were free.

I stood by the perimeter wire, a boundary no longer, with Cressida on my fist, as the heavily armed steel-helmeted Yanks poured into the camp. There was hand-shaking and back-slapping, and great boxes of the famous American K rations were unloaded. It was a moment to savour, like awakening from a long and terrible dream. The German guards had fled or had given themselves up, and we were now once more under the direct control of our S.B.O. The Americans, having set us free, drove onwards in relentless pursuit of their beaten and fleeing enemy. Occasional shots could be heard far to the east as they encountered scattered pockets of resistance, but this did not concern us.

We stood around in groups, trying to re-orientate ourselves; to realise that what we had yearned for, in some cases for five interminable years, had actually happened. We were free at last. The nagging uncertainty was over, and in the fullness of time we would return to the homes we had not seen for so many heart-aching years. We collected the boxes of rations bestowed upon us by our American liberators, and had the best feast most of us could remember. It was decided by the S.B.O. that we would have to wait in the camp, now our refuge was no longer a place of confinement, until the authorities decided what to do about us. We were allowed a modicum of liberty; we could go for walks in groups in the surrounding countryside.

We went out with Cressida, who may have felt something of the change in atmosphere, charged as it was with hidden depths of excitement. We passed through the main gates, which now stood invitingly open, and soon plunged into the surrounding woodlands. The first sound I heard was the gentle tripping cadence of a willow warbler, like a little musical waterfall. This has been to me ever since the sweetest and most welcoming of all bird songs. We found a tiny leaf-green tree frog clambering amongst the twigs of an alder tree. I stood in silence and marvelled at these things anew. Those who have never experienced the awfulness of years spent in the unreal, deeply frustrating half-world of a prison camp, will not fully realise the intense joy, the spiritual uplift which we felt in those first few, unforgettable, unforgotten hours of freedom regained. We did not talk about it; we just lived it, and that was all sufficient. Here we were, alive and free, with all of life before us. Cressida roused on my fist, her powerful feet took a firmer grip, and her lustrous dark eyes were alight with the happiness she too was feeling. She flew to a rotten stump and gave herself a thorough preening, while we lay back on a carpet of moss amongst the wood anemones, which stretched like scattered, wind-blown snowflakes beneath the silver birches.

A few days later we got the order we had been waiting for. Smart in new battle-dress drawn from the camp quartermaster's stores, kept in reserve for just such an occasion, we marched to the nearby airfield which, despite the continuous bombing, still remained serviceable. There, neatly lined up, stood a flight of Dakotas, ready to whisk us away from the scene of our captivity. An American war correspondent was there too, and he asked me a lot of questions about Cressida, who was later to become thoroughly blasé about Press conferences. We climbed aboard and soon we were airborne and on our way to Brussels.

I thought of my last air trip, in the J.U.52 carrying me wounded and dispirited from Bizerta to Palermo, nearly two years before. The lumbering Dakotas, for all their clumsy appearance, travelled fast and soon we had landed at Brussels Airport. We spent the night at the Caserne Aiguille, an old Belgian Army barracks; here for the first time we met English women in the form of Red Cross and F.A.N.Y.S. It was a strange sensation meeting them after two and a half years of an entirely monastic existence. However, we had a terrific reception, and Cressida came in for enough fuss and adulation to turn her head, but she accepted it with queenly condescension and obviously regarded it as her due.

The next morning, after a splendid breakfast of eggs and bacon, we took off once more, crossed the Channel, passed high above the white cliffs of Dover, and eventually landed at an airfield near Beaconsfield. Here again we had a great welcome from the R.A.F. Some of us, overcome with emotion, actually knelt and kissed the green English grass, a token of gratitude which we must all have felt to a considerable degree. We spent the night at a large country house amongst the woods and fields of Buckinghamshire; next morning we received some most welcome pay, ration cards, and all the usual paraphernalia connected with life in wartime Britain. Finally we were all given first-class railway warrants and sent on leave.

I travelled across London by taxi with Cressida perched on my fist, and felt as if I was in the midst of some sort of dream as we passed all the old familiar places I knew and loved so well. Marble Arch, Park Lane, Piccadilly, the Strand, and finally Charing Cross station, were all just as I remembered them in 1942. I sent a telegram to my mother to say we were coming. We climbed aboard the old well-loved train which meandered across the green pastures of the south on its way to Horam; the train I had caught so many times before when travelling from Bradfield or Gordonstoun, in the carefree days before the war. I remembered the familiar names of the stations, now blacked-out to confuse enemy parachutists; Hever, Tunbridge Wells, Edenbridge, Eridge, Mayfield, Heathfield, and at last Horam.

I took Cressida from her perch on the luggage rack and stepped out on to the platform. I had just begun my

walk towards the barrier when I was almost overwhelmed
by a hairy whirlwind. Bracken had covered the length of
the platform in a few elastic bounds; now she was all over
me, kissing me, leaping up to my chest and entwining
herself around my legs. I patted her and rubbed her
grizzled back as she reared up against my chest; her dark
eyes beneath her tousled eyebrows looked into mine, and
I was too overcome to say a word. My mother, laughing
and happy, joined us, and George the gardener was there
to drive us home.

It was a fine, sunny afternoon in late April as we had
our tea on the lawn under the scarlet oak, now green with
the promise of early spring. My mother and I lay in
deck-chairs; Bracken stretched at my feet, her eyes never

leaving my face. Cressida was sitting a few feet above us in the branches ticking happily, with a full crop, grabbing at leaves like a mischievous kitten, as happy to be home as I was to see her there. As I glanced up at her where she sat, russet amongst the green, I remembered the promise I had made on that December night in 1942, as the train swept us northward to Liverpool and the waiting troop-ship. I had kept that promise; I had brought her safely home.